AF376217

Dugout
to the Other Side –
Appendix

An Asmat song-text
transcribed and translated

Alexander de Antoni

Cuvillier Verlag
2013

Bibliografische Information der Deutschen Nationalbibliothek
Die Deutsche Nationalbibliothek verzeichnet diese Publikation in der Deutschen Nationalbibliografie; detaillierte bibliografische Daten sind im Internet über http://dnb.d-nb.de abrufbar.
1. Aufl. - Göttingen : Cuvillier, 2013

978-3-95404-414-6

Contents

1

Introduction

The first time I became acquainted with parts of the story of a person called Saunat was in 1984. He is a mythical hero of an Asmat subgroup living on the river Fayit in the southern area of the Asmat region. His memory is awakened by singing his story. This is sometimes practised during a sago feast or when it is quiet in the village because many inhabitants are out. It could well be that many of the men have gone into the jungle to harvest sago and to hunt or go fishing (de Antoni 2010[1]: 108).

During a stay in Basim in 1984, I was offered the opportunity to make a tape recording of a song dealing with some of the adventurous experiences Saunat was said to have had[2]. It was sung to the accompaniment of drumming by men from Naneu, a village further upstream along the Fayit. In the area of this river the Kaweinag language is spoken (de Antoni 2010[1]: 41).

Years later, in July and August 2007, a transcription and the translation of the song-texts were made in Basim. The results of the attempts to achieve these renditions of the recorded texts are documented here. The text of the stanzas of the song is rendered in a Kaweinag transcription and in two translations, into Indonesian and finally English.

---

[1] de Antoni, Alexander (2010). Dugout to the Other Side: Social structures inscribed in mythic tales and cosmological concepts of the Asmat. Göttingen: Cuvillier.

[2] The audio recordings of the mythic song are stored in form of a digital copy in the 'Phonogrammarchiv der Österreichischen Akademie der Wissenschaften' (PhAÖAW, Wien 1., Liebiggasse 5) together with other recordings in the collection 'Sammlung: de Antoni: West Papua 1984'. The recordings of the Saunat-song can be found under the following archive numbers: stanzas 1-11: D6680; stanzas 12-15: D6679; stanzas 16-29: D6678.

It may be seen as confusing that such a large number of translation variants is reproduced here. However, on closer examination, this form of representation may reveal new insights. As part of a comparative study of the various translations either one or the other turns out to be more a commentary on the original sung text than a translation. Identified as such, these sentences will prove to be of crucial help in interpreting the song and therefore to an authentic understanding of it. This fact represents a major reason for juxtaposing the diverse variants of the translation in a comparative form as is done here. In their diversity the versions contribute to a contextual understanding of the complete lyrics.

The text dealt with here corresponds to that used as a main source in my book 'Dugout to the Other Side'. In that paper it was entitled text '1b' (de Antoni 2010[1]: 61-87).

In the rendering of the representations of the text in the following chapter (2 - Text of the Saunat song), every line of the stanza of the song is reproduced in three versions as illustrated in the following explanatory note:

[X] *Transcription of the text of the song in the Kaweinag language made by Lukas Bayua from Biopis*

[X] Translation into Indonesian by Mateus Akin from Basim [Translation into Indonesian by Lukas Bayua] [Translation into Indonesian worked out by Lukas Bayua a few days after the previous translation (L.)] [Translation into Indonesian made by Petrus[3] from Basim (P.)] [Translation into Indonesian by an unknown translator assisted by Bavo Felndity[4] (?)]

[X] Translation of the Indonesian translation into English [Translation of the Asmat transcription of Lukas or of his Indonesian translation into English made by Lukas Bayua in collaboration with Bavo Felndity] [Translation of the later Indonesian translation of Lukas into English (L.)]

For a more detailed contextual description of the texts and their producers see my book (de Antoni 2010[1]: 49-59).

---

[3] Petrus is a boat-driver for Bavo Felndity, parish priest in Basim. Felndity wrote down the text as translated by Petrus.

[4] Bavo Felndity is Roman Catholic diocesan parish priest in Basim. He comes from the Tanimbar Islands and is therefore familiar with the Indonesian dialect spoken in these eastern parts of the country. He also speaks good English.

Working on the transcription of the song-text and the translations in 2007 in Basim, the collaborators expressed quite a number of remarkable comments. Together with remarks to the translation, these have been added to the text as notes in parentheses. In addition, question marks enclosed in brackets were inserted to mark questionable translations.

Alternative spellings of proper names as well as of animal species in the Asmat texts are reproduced in the translations according to the way they were spelled by the authors in the manuscripts. These original spellings could be of linguistic importance. They may possibly reveal clues to the local pronunciation of the expressions. "For example the apparently equivalent usage of Y and J as initials of proper names" (see Saunat 28:15,17,22) makes a more accurate reconstruction of the local pronunciation of these names possible. In this case, it could well be that the 'Y' is used to refer to the English consonantal allophone of this letter. Then writing 'J', the Dutch way of indicating the same pronunciation is addressed. In both cases, the pronunciation is the same. Consequently, a pronunciation of the name corresponding to that of 'Y' in the English word 'year' would be obvious.

Asmat are hardly very familiar with orthographic rules. In general, spelling as practised here is the result of adaptations to individual pronunciations and local writing customs (de Antoni 2010[1]: 59).

2

Text of the Saunat song

Stanza 1

[1] *Ya sana bati yanipi urumuna ya ini simara*
[1] Kali potong bagus sekali ujung ke ujung
[1] The connecting river is very beautiful from one end to the other. [Down there you cry with a soft voice there.]

[2] *ya sana Tayuruwiata bati yani Napiayoto urumuna ya*
[2] di bawah sana ada bunyi tangisan dari Tayuruwiata
[2] Down there exists a voice of crying of Tayuruwiata. [Down there Tayuruwiata cries with a sweet voice there.]

3 ini simara bati urumuna ya ini simara
[3] kedengaran bunyi itu indah sekali
[3] It sounds very beautiful. [Down there cries with a sweet voice there.]

[4] *ya jiwa ukunina pi ayoto sasinima ya ini simara*
[4] kali potong itu lurusnya bagaikan barisan burung
[4] The connecting river is straight like a row of birds. [Down there you cry with a sweet voice there.]

[5] *ya jiwa Naminiyoro uku ninapi ayoto sasinima*
[5] Naminiyoro kali potong itu sebaiknya harus dipakai terus
[5] Naminiyoro continues making use of the connecting river. [Down there Naminiyoru (left name of Tayuruwiata) cries for you with a sweet voice there.]

^{6} *ya ini simara Sawini kini fi fo metame basikini fi*
^{6} sedang datang Sawini ada bunyi datang terus
^{6} Sawini is coming, the voice is always coming [There Sawini has a deaf ear,
because of hunting a pig.]

^{7} *fometame Sawini kini fi fo metame basikini fi fometame.*
^{7} baik sekali.
^{7} very beautiful.

Stanza 2

^{1} *Sawini sapi yai bai rima osarame. Sawini sapi yai bai rima osarame. Sapi yai bai
rima usarame*
^{1} Sawini bunyi babi di air terus, Sawini bunyi babi di air terus, babi di perahu penuh
^{1} Sawini, the screaming of the pig in the water continuously, Sawini the screaming
of the pig in the water continuously, the canoe is full of pigs. [Sawini, the canoe
is full of cassowary, the canoe already full of cassowary.]

^{2} *bairame usrame: utua saka saka imarame*
^{2} di perahu penuh bunyi bunyi terus
^{2} The canoe full of screaming, continuous screaming. [Already full, a bird (*utua*)
makes 'saka-saka' there.]

^{3} *saki saka saka ima panime aku yaupi saku saka saka*
^{3} buring bangau bersuara dari atas kali Aku dan muaranya bubar dari situ
^{3} The silk-heron whistles over the river Aku and its mouth ending from there. [Saki
makes 'saka-saka' there in the mouth of the Aku-river 'saka-saka'.]

^{4} *ima pani me*
^{4} ada sedang datang bunyi burung dari atas
^{4} Just now the voice of a bird comes from above. [that's how it is.]

Stanza 3

[1] *Saunato uru u utani manauma mutafa Saunato uru u utani manauma mutafa tipa faka imara*

[1] Saunato engkau jago tombak babi, Saunato engkau jago tombak babi, kasih puas saya

[1] Saunato you pierce the pig with the spear well, Saunato you pierce the pig with the spear well, make me satisfied [Saunato, you have a pig-spear and it reaches the jungle of the river Manau. Saunato, you have a pig-spear and it reaches the jungle of the river Manau.]

[2] *Pisima muta tipa faka imare pisima muta tipa faka imareyanuma teirama*

[2] sampai di atas kali potong, sampai di atas kali potong, ambil anjing terus

[2] up to the connecting river, up to the connecting river, always take the dog with you. [It reaches in the jungle of river Pisi. It reaches in the jungle of river Pisi. Take the pig-spear.]

[3] *uru u uta nima yanuma teirame Sawini uru basi*

[3] Sawini engkau jago tombak babi lalu ambil anjing terus

[3] Sawini you pierce the pig with the spear well, then always take the dog with you. [You have the pig-spear and take a walk, Sawini.]

[4] *dukiri. Yanuma teirame Sawini uru basi dukiri. Yanuma teirame Sawini uru basi dukiri.*

[4] sambil perintah, Sambil perintah, Sambil perintah.

[4] Command at the same time, command at the same time, command at the same time, [You have a pig-spear. You have a pig-spear. You have a pig-spear.]

[5] *Akau mamutafa tipa fakaimare*

[5] sambil dayung ke atas kali potong

[5] while rowing up to the connecting river. [It reaches to the jungle of the river Akau.]

[6] *Yanuma teirame Sawini basi dukirima yanuma*

[6] sambil perintah saya dayung dengan Sawini

[6] Command, at the same time I row with Sawini. [Take and walk away Sawini, pig-spear and walk.]

[7] *teirame. Akau mamutafa tipa fakaimare*

[7] ujung dayungnya sampai di kali potong

[7] The point of the oar up to the connecting river, [Walk to the jungle of the river Akau,]

[8] *pisi mamutafa tifa fakaimare*

[8] ujung ujungnya habis di kali potong

[8] both of its points end in the connecting river. [to the jungle of river Pisi there.]

Stanza 4

[1] *Saunato datu suni Saunato datu suni wisima tifa*

[1] Saunato takut setan, Saunato takut setan di pinggir kali potong

[1] Saunato is afraid of the evil spirit, Saunato is afraid of the evil spirit on the bank of the connecting river. [Saunato is afraid of the evil spirit, Saunato is afraid of the evil spirit, until he reaches the shore of the short cut river.]

[2] *papira datu suni. Saunato datu suni wisisima*

[2] bunyian semua karena Saunato takut setan

[2] Everything sounds, because Saunato is afraid of the evil spirit. [He makes noise because he is afraid of the evil spirit. Saunato afraid of the evil spirit at the shore of the short cut river.]

[3] *tifa papira datu suni. Puma peisimara arpapa*

[3] semua kasih bunyi karena takut setan

[3] Everything sounds, because being afraid of the evil spirit, [He makes noise in the canoe because he is afraid of the evil spirit making him crazy,]

[4] *binipu. Pumape isimare puma pe isimare arpapa*

[4] menguasai pikiran semua orang di rumah

[4] dominates the thoughts of all people in the house, [make him crazy, make him crazy.]

[5] *binupu Pumape isimare Saunato datu suni*

[5] menguasai pikiran di tempat. Saunatu takut setan

[5] dominates the thoughts in the place. Saunatu is afraid of the evil spirit. [Make him crazy, Saunato afraid of evil spirit.]

[6] *Saunata datu suni fisima tipa papire datu suni*

[6] Saunata takut setan. Saunata jalan di pinggir kali potong

[6] Saunata is afraid of the evil spirit. Saunata walks on the bank of the connecting river. [Saunata is afraid of the evil spirit, afraid of the evil spirit till the short cut river.]

[7] Saunatu datusuni Saunato datusi wisima tifa papira

[7] Saunatu takut setan. Saunatu pergi tinggal di kali potong

[7] Saunatu is afraid of the evil spirit. Saunatu goes to live at the connecting river. [Saunatu afraid of the evil spirit, Saunato is afraid of evil spirit till the short cut river.]

[8] datu suni puma pe isimare arupa pa binupu puma pe

[8] hanya takut setan menguasai pikiran di tempat saja

[8] Only being afraid of the evil spirit dominates the thinking at this spot, [Afraid of evil spirit, makes him crazy and confused.]

[9] isimare puma pe isimare arupapa binupu puma pe

[9] berpikir terus seorang diri karena takut

[9] again and again thinking alone of the fear. [already crazy, already crazy.]

[10] ismare Sawina bi omere. Sawina biumare

[10] Sawina takut setan sawina sambil berteriak terus

[10] Sawina is afraid of the evil spirit, at the same time Sawina continues screaming. [Sawina afraid of evil spirit, Sawina afraid of evil spirit.]

[11] yaifa sima papire bi omere. Sawina biumare yaifa sima papire bi omere. Puma pe isimare

[11] semua orang takut, semua orang takut, takut di tempat

[11] All people are afraid, all people are afraid, are afraid at the place. [He makes noise because being crazy of that by drumming the sides of the canoe because afraid of evil spirit. He makes noise because being crazy of that by drumming the sides of the canoe because afraid of evil spirit.]

[12] Arpapa binupu pumape isimare arpapa binupu pumape

[12] dia hanya berpikir begitu terus dia hanya berpikir begitu terus

[12] He is constantly thinking of that, he is always thinking of that. [Already crazy, already crazy, already crazy.]

[13] isimare pumape isimare arpapa binupu puma pe isimare

[13] dia hanya berpikir begitu terus. Pikiran dia hanya seorang diri saja

[13] He is always thinking of that. His thoughts only of himself. [Already crazy, crazy, crazy.]

[14] *Sawina biumare Sawina biumare yaifa sima papire bi*
[14] Sawina takut setan. Sawina takut setan turun di perahu
[14] Sawina is afraid of the evil spirit. Sawina is afraid of the evil spirit, he steps down
into the canoe, [Sawina is afraid of evil spirit, Sawina is afraid of evil spirit,
makes noise by drumming on the sides of the canoe, afraid of evil spirit.]

[15] *omere biafapuma pe isimare.*
[15] Takut sendiri karena semua.
[15] alone afraid of everything. [crazy.]

Stanza 5

[1] *Dia ya jia umisimara*
[1] Ada bapak sambil teriak sepanjang malam terus
[1] There is father who screams continuously the whole night long. [Oh father, oh
dad, oh mama, oh mama.]

[2] *Awa dia ya jia umisimara awa ena ya jia umisimare.*
[2] aduh bapa yo sambil teriak, aduh mama yo sambil teriak
[2] Oh father, come scream at the same time, oh mother, come scream at the same
time. [Oh father, oh dad, oh mama, oh mama.]

[3] *Awa dia ya jia umisimare awa ena ya jia umisimare.*
[3] aduh bapa yo sambil teriak, aduh mama yo sambil teriak
[3] Oh father, come shout at the same time, oh mother, come shout at the same time.
[Oh father, oh dad, oh mama, oh mama.]

[4] *A enaya ya umisimare Tayuruwiata jiata Saunato*
[4] aduh mama yo sambil teriak Tayuruwiata jalan dengan Saunato
[4] Oh mother, come shout at the same time. Tayuruwiata goes with Saunato. [Oh my
mother, Tayuruwiata puts the child on the back of Saunato.]

[5] *memakifi pata ima puma isimare pata ima puma isimare*
[5] di ujung telinga setan tempel madu, setan tempel madu
[5] At the tip of the ear sticks the evil spirit with honey, the evil spirit sticks with
honey. [Put him on the back, put him on the back.]

[6] *Tayuruwita jiata Saunato bikifa pata ima puma*
[6] Tayuruwiata sudah tempel Saunato di belakang
[6] Tayuruwiata has already stuck Saunato on the back. [Tayuruwiata puts the child
on the back of Saunato, puts the child on the back.]

16

[7] *isimare pata ima puma isimare. Awa dia ya ya jia umisi*
[7] sambil tempel dia berteriak aduh bapa, teriak terus
[7] During the sticking he shouts 'oh father', continues shouting, [Put the child on the back, oh dad.]

[8] *mara awa enaya ya umisimare akia awaya umisimare*
[8] aduh, mama yo, dia teriak terus. Aduh kakak dia teriak terus
[8] Oh mother, come, he continues screaming. Oh older brother, he screams on. [Oh mama yo, Oh mama yo.]

[9] *awa usaka ya umisimare Naminiyoru maniaata*
[9] aduh tete yo, aduh nenek yo Naminiyoru teriak terus
[9] Oh grandfather, come, oh grandmother, come, Naminiyoru continues screaming. [He screams, Oh grandmother, Namininyoru put the child]

[10] *Sawini bikifa daisa puma isimare daisa puma isimare*
[10] Sawini madu hancur di belakang. Semua madu hancur di belakang
[10] Sawini the honey on the back is ruined. All the honey on the back is ruined. [on the back of Sawini, put it on his back, put it on his back.]

[11] *Naminiyoru maniaata Sawini daisima puma umisimara*
[11] Naminiyoru tempel madu di belakang Sawini
[11] Naminiyoru sticks honey on the back of Sawini. [Naminiyoru put the child on the back of Sawini, put it on the back.]

[12] *Daisa puma isimare awa awaya jaumisimara. Awa usaka*
[12] aduh mama yo dia sudah tempel di belakang saya. Aduh tete yo
[12] Oh mum, come. She has already stuck on my back. Oh grandfather, come. [Put it on the back, O mama yo, Oh mama yo.]

[13] *jaumisimare.*
[13] dia berteriak sepanjang malam terus.
[13] He/She shouts all the night through. [Oh grandma.]

Stanza 6

[1] *Itua ya paitemare tia amani Tayuruwiata*
[1] Sepanjang malam Tayuruwiata dibesarkan terus
[1] All the night long Tayuruwiata was enlarged further, [The crocodile is making a nest in the womb of Tayuruwiata.]

[2] *tua ayumura mara tua ayumura marini etua ayumura*
[2] besar terus sepanjang hari dan waktu
[2] even larger every day and all the time. [She likes raising the crocodile nest. She
    likes raising the crocodile nest.]

[3] *marini tia amani Bintutua (Bintutua=Waratutua) ayamura marini itua ya*
[3] mau dibesarkan dalam perut Bintutua (=ular naga)(=Ulat patda taksasa)
[3] Want to be enlarged in the belly of Bintutua (= snake-dragon) (worm *patda?*
    taksasa?) [She raises the nest Bintutua in her womb. She likes raising the
    crocodile nest.]

[4] *paitimare tia amani bintutua ya paitemare*
[4] batang itu ada dalam perut Bintutua
[4] The stem is in the belly of Bintutua. [Making Bintutua's nest in her womb,
    making the nest.]

[5] *Sawinatu we yaitua. Sawinato wi yaitu Sawinatu*
[5] Sawinatu orang yang bagus. Sawinato orang yang bagus. Sawinatu
[5] Sawinatu is a handsome human. Sawinato is a handsome human. Sawinatu
    [Sawinatu is a mad man, Sawinato a mad man. He is not a good man.]

[6] *putaka we yaitu. Sawinato wi yaitu Sawinatu putaka we yaitu.*
[6] orang yang tidak baik. Sawinatu orang yang tidak baik
[6] is not a good human. Sawinatu is not a good human. [He is a crazy man, he is a
    crazy man.]

[7] *Bevaka tua ya pai temara Waratutua*
[7] orang yang tidak baik suka buka mulut
[7] A bad human likes to open the mouth. [Crocodile nest, nest of Waratutua.]

[8] *ya pai temare yaiamani*
[8] di dalam perahu juga dia bersarang
[8] Also in the canoe he nests. [He makes nest in the womb.]

[9] *Bintutua ayu mura marini waratutua ayumura*
[9] Bintutua besarkan sarang dalam perut Waratutua
[9] Bintutua enlarges the nest in the belly of Waratutua. [Bintutua wants to make a
    nest, Waratutua makes a nest.]

[10] *marine waratutua ayu mura marine Sawini bisa*
[10] Sawini meninggalkan sarang Waratutua
[10] Sawini leaves the nest of Waratutua. [Waratutua makes a nest, Sawini makes a
nest.]

[11] *isratu Sawini putaka bisa yusra tua*
[11] Sawini langsung lurus pergi ke sarang
[11] Sawini walks directly to the nest. [Sawini makes such bad things, he is crazy.]

Stanza 7

[1] *Bi yakara ya umisamara wi bi yakara yaumisimare*
[1] Ada muka orang di situ sepanjang malam, ada muka orang di situ sepanjang
malam [Ada air di situkah, ada air di kali potongkah?]
[1] There is the whole night through a human face there, the whole night through
there is a human face there. [Is there water there, is there water in the
connecting river?]

[2] *Tayuruwiata sairima yapuma wimisimare wibisai rima ya*
[2] Tayuruwiata sambil pesan coba lihat muka orang itu [Tayuruwiata bilang jangan
ada air di kali potong, jangan ada air di kali potong.]
[2] During the message Tayuruwiata tries to look at the face of this human,
[Tayuruwiata says that there should be no water over there in the connecting
river, there should be no water in the connecting river.]

[3] *pua umisimare okami yakara yatwimisimare*
[3] sepanjang malam sambil jalan dia pesan ini [Ada air di kali potongkah? Ada air di
kali potongkah?]
[3] all the night during the walking he proclaims [Is there water in the connecting
river? Is there water in the connecting river?]

[4] *tauwia ura mi yakara ya umisimare Naminiyoru*
[4] Naminiyoru ada dengan air di situ [Ada air di kali potongkah? Tanya Naminiyoru]
[4] Naminiyoru is there with water. [Is there water in the connecting river, asks
Naminiyoru.]

[5] *ataruma yapua umisimare.*
[5] lempar dia ke dalam malam. [Mereka mengeluh karena tidak ada air.]
[5] Throw him into the night. [They complain to her because of the lack of water.]

Stanza 8

[1] *Sawinatu upi pumorufa tapa yaura pua isime.*

[1] Sawinatu menjadi orang di atas pohon sepanjang malam. [Sawinatu menjelma sebagai burung „Upipamorufa", sudah jadi.]

[1] Sawinatu becomes a human on the tree all night long. [Sawinatu transforms himself into the bird Upipamorufa, has already happened.]

[2] *Sawinatu upi pumorufa tapa yaura pua isime.*

[2] Sawinatu menjadi orang di atas pohon sepanjang malam. [Sawinatu menjelma sebagai burung „Upipamorufa", sudah jadi.]

[2] Sawinatu becomes a human on the tree all night long. [Sawinatu transforms himself into the bird Upipamorufa, has already happened.]

[3] *Tamatapisi pa omeifa tapa dara esa ini mia*

[3] Tamutapis(= perkumpulan roh dari perempuan yang mati melahirka)(kuntilanak?) sambil jalan dan makan. [Engkau naik ke rumah perempuan-perempuan yang mati melahirkan dan makan makanan mereka yang tidak kita kenal.]

[3] Tamutapis (= community of spirits of women who died after a delivery, evil female spirits) walks and eats at the same time. [You climb up to the house of the women who died at a birth and eat their food which we don't know.]

[4] *ume yifa tapa yaura es ini mi Tamatapisi tu omeijifa*

[4] Tamutapis sambil jalan dan makan sepanjang malam [Kita tidak tahu engkau naik ke rumah mereka, makan makanan mereka yang enak, ulat sagu yang enak.]

[4] Tamutapis, walking she/he eats the whole night through. [We don't know it. You climb up into their/her house and eat their/her good food, sago grubs.]

[5] *tapa dera ese ini mia umeifa tapa yau ra esa ini mia*

[5] mungkin mereka makan daun dan jadi daun [Makan makanan mereka yang tidak kita kenal, gemuk babi dan apa yang kau pernah makan di situ.]

[5] Possibly they eat a leaf and become a leaf. [Eats their/her food, which we don't know, pigs fat and what you already have eaten there.]

[6] *Saunatu upi pumarufa tapa yaura esa inimia upi puma*

[6] Saunatu menjadi orang di atas pohon sepanjang malam [Saunatu jadi burung Upipamorufa kami tidak tahu.]

[6] Saunatu becomes a human on a tree all night long, [Saunatu is transformed into the bird Upipamorufa. We don't know it.]

[7] *rufa tapa yau ra esa ini mia tapa yaura esa ini mia*

[7] sepanjang jadi orang di atas pohon terus [Engkau jadi burung Upipamorufa kami tidak tahu. Engkau jadi burung Upipamorufa kami tidak tahu.]

[7] becomes a human on a tree. [You are transformed into the bird Upipamorufa, we don't know it. You became the bird Upipamorufa, we don't know it.]

[8] *tapa yaura esa inimi Saunatu upi mumuru fa tapa*

[8] Saunatu karena makan daun jadi orang di atas [Engkau jadi burung kami tidak tahu Saunatu engkau jadi burung kami tidak tahu.

[8] Saunatu, because he eats a leaf, becomes a human up here, [You became a bird, we don't know it. Saunatu you became a bird, we don't know it.]

[9] *yaura esa ini mia. Tia pisi isu tamia manifa tapa yaura*

[9] menjadi roh dari perempuan mati hamil [Engkau jadi burung, engkau masuk rumah perempuan-perempuan mati melahirkan kami tidak tahu.]

[9] becomes a spirit of woman who died during the pregnancy, [You became the bird Upipamorufa, you arrive at the house of the women who died during a birth, we don't know it.]

[10] *Esa ini mia basi omere tapa yaura omsa ini mia.*

[10] mungkin menjadi babi betina. [Engkau makan gemuk babi kami tidak tahu, engkau makan gemuk babi kami tidak tahu.]

[10] maybe becomes a sow. [You eat pig's fat, we don't know it. You eat pig's fat, we don't know it.]

Stanza 9

[1] *Saunatu Taiyuruwiata tani ayatuaita purare*

[1] Saunatu coba lihat vagina Tayuruwiata bagus [Saunatu melihat kemaluan Tayuruwiata bagus.]

[1] Saunatu, have a look, the vagina of Tayuruwiata is beautiful. [Saunatu looks at the beautiful genital of Tayuruwiata.]

[2] *tani wami ji ema pumare sayifa erema pumare*

[2] dia kasih irisan bekas pada puki (puki=vagina) [Dia iris kemaluan dengan kampak, dia iris.]

[2] He makes a forming cut on the vagina. [He opens the vagina with a cut with an axe, he cuts open.]

[3] *Saunato Tairuwiata tani ayatufa apu rare*

[3] Saunato melihat puki Tayuruwiata bagus [Saunato melihat kemaluan Tayuruwiata bagus.]

[3] Saunato sees the beautiful vagina of Tayuruwiata. [Saunatu looks at the beautiful vagina of Tayuruwiata.]

[4] *tani wami ji imapumare sayifa erema pumare.*

[4] dia kasih irisan bekas pada puki. [Dia iris kemaluan dengan kampak, dia iris.]

[4] He makes a forming cut on the vagina. [He opens the vagina with a cut with an axe, he cuts open.]

[5] *Ayia duru tani du fe. Ayia duru tani du fe. Saunatu Taiyuruata tauta*

[5] Aduh saya punya puki dan pantat, aduh saya punya puki dan pantat, Saunatu teriak Tayuruwiata [Aduh saya punya kemaluan dan pantat. Aduh saya punya kemaluan dan pantat. Saunatu punya maitua Tayuruwiata.]

[5] Oh! my vagina and my bottom, Oh! my vagina and my arse, Saunatu shouts Tayuruwiata. [Au, my vagina and my bottom. Au, my vagina and my bottom. Tayuruwiata is the wife of Saunatu.]

[6] *aya tu fa aita purare tania wamijifa emapu*

[6] puki yang bagus sekali saya lihat itu [Punya kemaluan bagus, dia iris.]

[6] The most beautiful vagina that I see, [She has a beautiful vagina. He cuts it open.]

[7] *mare sayifa ema pumare Saunato Taiyuruwiata*

[7] Saunato kasih irisan bekas pada dia [Iris dengan kampak Saunato punya maitua Tayuruwiata.]

[7] Saunato gives a forming cut. [Cuts open with an axe, Saunatos wife is Tayuruwiata.]

[8] *tauta ayatufa aitapurare sayierema pumare*

[8] dia lihat perempuan karena bagus dengan irisan [Dia melihat bagus, dia iris dengan kampak.]

[8] He looks because of her beautiful cut, [He looks at the beauty, he cuts open with an axe.]

[9] *aita purare tani ofe ji ima pumare sayi fa erema*

[9] kasih bekas dengan buluh tajam karena bagus / enak [dia melihat kemaluan dan iris dengan kulit siput, iris dengan kampak.]

[9] gives a forming with a sharp bamboo chip, because it is pleasant. [He looks at the vagina and cuts it open with the shell of a mussel, cuts open with the axe.]

[10] *pumare. Aia dutani du fea aia du tani du fe*

[10] aduh saya puki dan pantat [Aduh saya punya kemaluan dan pantat, aduh saya punya kemaluan dan pantat.]

[10] Oh! I vagina and bottom, [Au, my vagina and bottom. Au, my vagina and bottom.]

[11] *Sawini damini yoro wiri ayatufa aita purare taiji*

[11] Sawini engkau buat Naminiyoru mati itu baik [Sawini melihat Naminiyoru cantik, dia iris dengan kulit siput.]

[11] Sawini, you kill Naminiyoru, it is good. [Sawini looks at the beautiful Naminiyoru, he cuts open with the mussel shell.]

[12] *ima pumare borafa eremapumare aia duru wiri*

[12] bapa kenapa tidak buat saya kampak [Dia belah iris dengan kampak, dia lihat pantat.]

[12] Father, why don't you make an axe for me. [He cuts open with an axe. He looks at the bottom.]

[13] *du asapi Naminiyoro wiri ayatufa aita purare*

[13] saya melihat Naminiyoru dari belakang saya menyesal [Dia lihat kemaluan Naminiyoru bagus.]

[13] I see Naminiyoru from the back side, I am sorry. [He looks at the beautiful vagina of Naminiyoru.]

[14] *wiri taijiima pumare borafa erema pumare.*

[14] laki-laki yang buat bukan perempuan. [Dia iris kemaluan dengan kampak, dia iris dengan kampak.]

[14] Men do that, not woman. [He cuts open the vagina with an axe. He cuts open with an axe.]

Stanza 10

[1] *Saunatu fekuria fekuri tumi biki fekuri fekuria*

[1] Saunatu lari pergi ke belakang rumah, lari pergi

[1] Saunatu runs away to the back of the house, runs away. [Saunatu goes, goes to the back of his home, goes, goes.]

[2] *Saunatu jirawa tami biki fekuria*

[2] Saunatu seorang yang tinggi lari ke belakang

[2] Saunatu the tall man, runs to the back. [Saunatu is a tall man, to the back of his house he goes.]

³ *Taiyuruwiata ayare ipiri duru fa ema kusumumare. Taiyuruwiata ayare ipiri duru fa ema kusumumare.*

³ ujung cawat Tayuruwiata saya buka. Ujung cawat Tayuruwiata saya buka.

³ I open the point of the loin-cloth of Tayuruwiata. [Tayuruwiata opens her grass skirt in front of me. Tayuruwiata opens her grass skirt in front of me.]

⁴ *Taiyuruwiata ayare ipiri duru fa ema kusumumare.*

⁴ Ujung cawat Tayuruwiata saya buka.

⁴ I open the point of the loin-cloth of Tayuruwiata. [Tayuruwiata opens her grass skirt in front of me,]

⁵ *durufa ema kusumumare Sawini fekuri fekuri*

⁵ di depan saya dia buka cawat Sawini pergi ke belakang

⁵ In front of me she opens her loin-cloth, goes to the back, [opens it in front of me and Sawini goes, goes.]

⁶ *Tami miki fekuri tami biki fekuri fekuri Sawini isu*

⁶ ke belakang rumah saya pergi. Pergi terus

⁶ I go to the back of the house. Go on, [To the back of your house, goes, goes to the back of the house, Sawini goes,]

⁷ *biki sauakuri sauakuri sauakuri sauni jirawa*

⁷ lompat, lompat, lompat di belakang karena tinggi

⁷ jumping, jumping, jumping back because of the tallness, [goes, goes, goes, tall Sawini goes from the back of the house,]

⁸ *isu biki sauakuri Naminiyaro sana ipiri durufa*

⁸ lompat di belakang rumah Naminiyoru

⁸ jumping to the back of the house of Naminiyoru. [goes, Tayuruwiata open your grass skirt for me!]

⁹ *ema kusumimare durufa ema furumumare*

⁹ di depan saya dia buka cawat pergi ke belakang

⁹ In front of me she opens her loin-cloth, goes to the back, [She begins to open her skirt for me and begins to open.]

¹⁰ *Naminiyoru saina ipiri duru fa ema furumumare.*

¹⁰ Naminiyoru buka cawat untuk saya

¹⁰ Naminiyoru opens the loin-cloth for me. [Naminiyoru begins to open her grass skirt for me.]

[11] *Naminiyoru saina ipiri durufa ema furumumare*
[11] Naminiyoru yang sebenarnya yang harus saya mau
[11] Naminiyoru is the one I have to desire. [Naminiyoru begins to open her grass
skirt for me.]

[12] *Naminiyoro saina ipiri durufa ema furumumare*
[12] Naminiyoru yang sebenarnya yang harus saya mau
[12] Naminiyoru is the one I have to desire. [Naminiyoru begins to open her grass
skirt for me.]

[13] *Durufa ema furumumare Naminiyoru saina ipiri.*
[13] kepada saya saja saya mau Naminiyoru buka
[13] Only to me I wanted, Naminiyoru opens. [Open in front of me, Naminiyoru
opens her grass skirt,]

[14] *Durufa ema furumumare ema furumumare.*
[14] kepada saya saja dia mau
[14] Only to me she wanted. [opens in front of me, opens in front of me.]

[15] *Sawini sauakuri sauakuri isu bikifa sauakuri*
[15] Sawini ke belakang terus, ke belakang terus
[15] Sawini goes further to the back, further to the back, [Sawini goes from the back
of the house,]

[16] *sauakuri isu bikifa sauakuri.*
[16] ke belakang terus cepat-cepat ke belakang rumah.
[16] on to the back, quickly to the back of the house. [goes from the back of the
house.]

Stanza 11

[1] *Faitipi unam basuayatui itibare ya Faitipi unam*
[1] Awan di atas kali (=sungai) Fayit bagus sekali
[1] The cloud over the river Fayit is very beautiful. [In the morning clouds over the
river Fayit look beautiful, clouds over the river Fayit.]

[2] *basuaya tu tamenimi yaiti bare ya Faitipi unambasu*
[2] barisan awan terlalu bagus di atas Fayit
[2] The file of clouds is beautiful over the Fayit, [The sun looks beautiful through the
clouds over the river Fayit.]

3 ayato tame nimi yaiti bare ya Faitipi unam basu ayato

3 bagusnya seperti jajaran barisan rumah

3 their beauty is like the row of houses. [The clouds over the river Fayit stand in
    order and it is beautiful.]

4 tame nimi yaiti bare Saunato oro tara isa pisi

4 kelihatan terlalu bagus Saunato engkau lihat itu

4 It looks so nice, Saunato do you see it. [In the morning Saunato has a sister.]

5 tapisi bati bata wimi timasi Saunato uru ubati fa

5 perempuan semua menangis karena babi Saunato

5 All women cry because of the pig Saunato. [In the morning women cry because of
    Saunato. They cry because of you.]

6 bata wimi timasi Saunatu uru tara isapisi batifa bata

6 mama Saunatu semua menangis terus

6 The mother of Saunatu, all carry on crying, [That morning they are still crying
    because of Saunatu. Your sisters still crying because of you.]

7 wimi timase Saunatu yuri u batifa bata wimi tima

7 menangis karena Saunato jago pergi berburu dengan anjing

7 crying, because Saunato, the hero goes hunting with a dog. [Still crying for
    Saunatu. They remember the dog that hunts pigs.]

8 se ya faitipi unam basuayato tame nimi ya wimi timare

8 semua awan di atas Fayit semua bagus

8 All clouds over the Fayit they are all beautiful, [The clouds over the river Fayit are
    really beautiful.]

9 ya faitipi unam basu ayato tame nimi ya wimi

9 indah sekali awan semua

9 so beautiful are all clouds. [The clouds over the river Fayit are really beautiful.]

10 timare yaimipi so basuayato aima wimi timare ya

10 saya melihat semua awan indah

10 I see all beautiful clouds, [The clouds over the river Fayit are really beautiful.]

11 jimipi sori basu ayato tame nimi ya wimitimare

11 semua awan indah dan merah seperti jambu

11 all clouds are beautiful and red just like a *jambu* fruit. [The clouds over the river
    Fayit are really beautiful.]

26

¹² *yajimi so basuayato toroto yawimi timare*
¹² awan-awan indah sekali dan saya sedih
¹² The clouds are beautiful and I am sad. [The sunshine through the clouds is very
    beautiful.]

¹³ *Saunato oro yakumen yoara imani taua wi*
¹³ saudara-saudari Saunato semua sedih
¹³ The siblings of Saunato are all sad. [Saunato, your *yakumen*-sister cries for you.]

¹⁴ *mi ti mase Sawini ara basi imani taua wimi*
¹⁴ semua menangis Sawini terus
¹⁴ All carry on crying Sawini, [They cry for your pig, they are still crying till this
    morning,]

¹⁵ *tima se.*
¹⁵ serentak menangis.
¹⁵ crying at the same time. [this morning.]

Stanza 12

¹ *Saunatu faitipi yawi basu ayato aenawa aitimare*
¹ Saunatu sinar matahari dari udik Fayit bagus
¹ Saunatu the sunbeam from the side of the Fayit is beautiful. [Saunatu, upstream
    the Fayit the sunrise is coming.]

² *yuri baridu ataya umtaorae Saunato faitipi*
² anjing dayung dengan cepat tangan Saunato
² The dog rows quickly, the hand of Saunato. [Take your dog and the oar and leave
    to the upper course of the Fayit.]

³ *yawi basu ayato anaoaaitimare yuri bari pu ayato*
³ sambil berburu sinar matahari bagus, anjing dayung
³ During the hunting the sunbeam is beautiful, the dog is rowing. [The sun with
    good clouds is coming. Take the dog and the oar and go away.]

⁴ *ata ye umto oraye tamina ameitimare dasna*
⁴ taru di depan saya hasil yang baik
⁴ Lay in front of me the best yield. [Row and go away. Take your dog. Your penis is
    uncovered.]

5 tamina ameitimare tamina ameitimare dasna

5 saya pergi ke rumah nanti kosong

5 I walk later on empty into the hut. [You get up naked, you get up naked.]

6 tamina amaitimare Saunato faitipi yawi basu

6 Saunato dayung sambil buka dada

6 Saunato rows with his naked breast. [You get up naked Saunato upstream Fayit. The sun is shining well.]

7 ayato aenawa aitimare yuri bari pu ayato

7 sambil dayung anjing di perahu

7 While rowing the dog is in the canoe. [The sun is coming. Take the dog and row and go away. Take the dog, row and go away. It is good.]

8 ataye um taoraye tamina ameitimare

8 silahkan naik ke atas rumah saya

8 Please come up into my house. [You go away. You get up and go away.]

9 Tamina amejitimare. Tamina amejitimare. Tamina amejitimare. Sawini yo basuayato

9 sinar matahari masuk rumah, sinar matahari masuk rumah, sinar matahari masuk rumah. Sawini awan bagus

9 The sunbeam comes into the house, the sunbeam comes into the house, the sunbeam comes into the house. Sawini the cloud is beautiful, [You get up and it is good. You get up and it is good. You get up and it is good. Sawini the sunshine is good.]

10 aenawa aitimare esona ameitimare

10 sedang datang di rumah semua terang

10 just comes into the house, everything is illuminated. [She (the sun) is coming. So you get up. The house is still there.]

11 dasna isuna ameitimare dasna isuna ameitimare

11 barisan rumah barisan rumah bagus sekali

11 The row of houses, the row of houses is very beautiful. [That house is empty. It is still empty.]

12 dasna isuna ameitimare Saunato faitipi

12 rumah di atas Fayit kosong semua.

12 The house over the Fayit is completely empty. [That house is still empty. Saunato upstream the Fayit.]

[13] *yawi basu ayato anawa aitimare airibari*
[13] sinar matahari indah sekali dari arah sana
[13] The sunbeam is very beautiful from the direction over there. [The sunshine is
    good. It is coming. Go for pig-hunting.]

[14] *pari ayato ata ye umta ora ye esuna ameitimare*
[14] tolong dayung dulu di atas perahu ini
[14] Please help rowing this canoe. [Row away, you try to go. The house is still empty.]

[15] *dasna isuna ameitimare Sawini yimipi yasuru*
[15] semua kayu di atas kali Fayit kosong karena Sawini
[15] All the wood is empty close to the river upstream Fayit because of Sawini.
    [Sawini, the sun upstream.]

[16] *basu ayato aenawa aitimare airi pari ayato*
[16] barisan awan di atas air juga indah sekali
[16] The row of clouds over the water is also very beautiful, [The clouds in the
    morning are coming. Pig-hunting is good.]

[17] *ataye umta rai*
[17] sambil dayung terus.
[17] continuing to row at the same time. [You row away.]

Stanza 13

[1] *Saunato yaka yapi mana ye tipmaorai*
[1] Saunato coba lihat di atas sana. [Saunato coba lihat di atas (L.)]
[1] Saunato try once to look up there. [Saunat lift up your eyes and look!] [Saunato
    tries to look upwards. (L.)]

[2] *ya Fayiti yaopi ma na ye tipmarai Saunato yaka yapi*
[2] coba lihat di atas kali Fayit Saunato coba [lihat di atas Fayit (L.)]
[2] Try once Saunato to look at the river the upper course of the Fayit, try it, [Look at
    the Fayit upstream, Saunato.] [Look up the river. (L.)]

[3] *mana ye tipmarai yaka Fayiti yaope mana ye*
[3] lihat di atas kali Fayit
[3] look at the river to the upper course of the Fayit. [Look there up the Fayit river.]
    [Saunato tries to look up. (L.)]

[4] *tipmarai.*

[4] tapi harus dari sini

[4] But it has to be from here. [Look!] [The Fayit upriver, try to look. (L.)]

[5] *Saunatu yaka yapi mana ja tipmarai*

[5] Saunatu coba lihat di atas sana [Saunato coba lihat di atas (L.)]

[5] Saunatu, try to look up there. [Saunato, try to lift up your eyes and look up.] [Saunato tries to look upwards. (L.)]

[6] *yaka Fayiti yapi mana ja tipmarai*

[6] coba lihat di atas kali Fayit. Saunato coba [lihat di atas Fayit (L.)]

[6] Try once to look at the river up the river Fayit, Saunato, try it. [Look at the battle upriver.] [Looks at the river Fayit upwards. (L.)]

[7] *Sawina yaka yapi mana ja tipmarai*

[7] Sawina coba lihat tapi harus dari sini [Saunato coba lihat di atas (L.)]

[7] Sawina try to look at it, but it must be from here. [Sawina try to lift up your eyes and look up.] [Saunato tries to look upwards. (L.)]

[8] *yaka Fayiti yapi mana ye tipmarai*

[8] coba lihat di atas kali Fayit. Saunato coba. [di atas Fayit coba lihat (L.)]

[8] Try once at the river at the upper course of the Fayit, Saunato, try it, [Look at the battle upriver.] [Tries to look up the Fayit. (L.)]

[9] *Sawina yawiaimumara yaka fati yapimana ya*

[9] Sawina melihat ini ada dari atas [Saunatu matahari ada datang di atas Fayit (L.)]

[9] Sawina looks at it from above. [Saunatu, look the sun is coming from upstream Fayit.] [Saunatu, the sun rises over the Fayit. (L.)]

[10] *tipmarai Fayiti yapi mana ya tipmarai*

[10] coba lihat di atas kali Fayit. Saunato coba [coba lihat di atas Fayit (L.)]

[10] Try once to look at the river at the upper course of the Fayit. [Try to look up the river Fayit.] [Try to look up the Fayit (L.)]

[11] *Yumi atamu ta tumina aitimare Sarai atamu*

[11] suara burung sarai bersuara karena pagi [Yumi bersuara Sarai bersuara (L.)]

[11] The voice of the Sarai bird sings because of the morning. [Yumi (name of a bird) shows her voice and Sarai (bird) shows her voice.] [Yumi shows her voice and Sarai shows her voice. (L.)]

[12] *ta tumina aitimare Yumi atamu ta tumina*

[12] burung-burung ini senang dengan bersuaro [Sarai bersuara Yumi bersuara (L.)]

[12] These birds enjoy singing. [They are showing their voice and Yumi shows her voice.] [Sarai utters a sound, Yumi utters a sound. (L.)]

[13] *aitimare sarai atamu ta tumina aitimara*

[13] suara burung sarai berseru terus semuanya indah [Yumi bersuara Sarai bersuara (L.)]

[13] The voice of the bird Sarai keeps on calling, everything is beautiful. [Sarai is showing her voice, they are showing their voices.] [Yumi utters a sound, Sarai utters a sound. L.)]

[14] *Sawini yaka Jimipi amai ye tipmarai*

[14] Sawini coba lihat ke atas kali Fayit [Saunato coba lihat di atas Fayit (L.)]

[14] Sawini, try once to look at the river at the upper course of the Fayit. [Sawini tries to look up the river Jimipi (=Fayit).] [Saunato tries to look up the Fayit. (L.)]

[15] *Jimipi yasuru basu ayato aenawa aitimare*

[15] sinar matahari di atas kali itu baik [Matahari di atas Fayit ada datang (L.)]

[15] The sunbeam over the river is good. [The sun is coming upstream Jimipi.] [The sun rises over the Fayit. (L.)]

[16] *Sawini aenawa aitimare Jimipi yasuru*

[16] Sawini heran sinar matahari dari atas [Sawini mau datang matahari di atas Fayit (L.)]

[16] Sawini is suprised of the sunbeam from above. [Sawini, the sun is coming from upstream Jimipi.] [Sawini, the sun wants to rise over the Fayit. (L.)]

[17] *basu ayato anawa aitimare*

[17] sinar matahari kelihatan baik sekali [sinar matahari mau datang (L.)]

[17] The sunbeam looks so good. [The clouds in the sky appear upstream and are beautiful.] [Sunshine wants to come. (L.)]

[18] *Akumi imani tewasia aitimara*

[18] suara burung Akumi terdengar merdu [Yumi bersuara (L)]

[18] The voice of the Akumi bird sounds sonorous. [Akumi (left name of Yumi) is crying sadly.] [Yumi raises her voice. (L.)]

[19] *kakau imani tewasia aitimara*

[19] suara burung pombo hitam ikut terdengar [Sarai bersuara (L.)]

[19] You can hear the voice of the black Pombo-bird. [Kakau (left name of Sarai) is crying sadly.] [Sarai raises her voice. (L.)]

Stanza 14

[1] *Saunatu pu sina tika irima osare*
[1] Saunatu tanam dayung di lumpur [Saunatu pergi tanam dayung (L.)]
[1] Saunatu plants the oar in the mud, [Saunatu goes to plant his oar in the mud.]
    [Saunatu to plant the oar, (L.)]

[2] *Fayiti yaupu pusina tika irima osara*
[2] Tanam dayung di muara kali Fayit [pergi tanam dayung di muara Fayit (L.)]
[2] plants the oar in the mouth of the river Fayit. [Go to plant the oar downstream the
    Fayit.] [plant the oar in the mouth of the Fayit. (L.)]

[3] *Saunatu pusina teka irima osara*
[3] Saunatu tanam dayung di lumpur [Saunatu pergi tanam dayung (L.)]
[3] Saunatu plants the oar in the mud, [Saunatu goes to plant his oar in the mud.]
    [Saunatu goes to plant the oar, (L.)]

[4] *Fayiti yaupu pusina teka irima osara*
[4] Tanam dayung di muara kali Fayit [pergi tanam dayung di muara Fayit (L.)]
[4] plants the oar in the mouth of the river Fayit. [Go to plant the oar downstream the
    Fayit.] [plant the oar in the mouth of the Fayit. (L.)]

[5] *yawi yara seja wimi timara*
[5] matahari cepat terbit sambil di perahu [Matahari coba datang cepat (L.)]
[5] The sun rises quickly, by the side of the canoe. [The sun comes up quickly.] [Sun
    please come quickly. (L.)]

[6] *Fayiti yawi yara se jawi mi timara Fayiti yawi*
[6] matahari di atas kali Fayit cepat datang. Matahari Fayit cepat [Matahari di atas
    Fayit coba datang cepat]
[6] The sun over the river Fayit comes quickly. The sun Fayit is fast. [Sun of river
    Fayit come quickly. Sun of river Fayit come quickly.] [Sun over the Fayit
    please come quickly. (L.)]

[7] *yara se ja wimi timara yawi yara seja*
[7] suara burung cepat matahari datang [Matahari cepat datang cepat datang (L.)]
[7] The sun over the river Fayit comes quickly. The sun Fayit is fast. [First of all,
    come sun.] [come sun, come quickly, come sun, come quickly. (L.)]

[8] *wimi timara Fayiti yawi yara se ja*
[8] sambil minta matahari Fayit dia duduk
[8] While asking for the sun Fayit he is sitting. [The sun up the river Fayit comes quickly. The sun up the river Fayit comes quickly.]

[9] *wimi timara Saunatu yawi jara seja wimi*
[9] Saunatu tidur di perahu tidak terasa
[9] Saunatu is sleeping unconsciously in the canoe, [Saunatu, ask the sun to come quickly.]

[10] *timara*
[10] cepat sudah
[10] quick already.

[11] *Sawini pusini teka irima osare Fayiti yaupu*
[11] Sawini tanam dayung di lumpur di muara Fayit
[11] Sawini plants the oar in the mud at the mouth of the Fayit. [Sawini goes to plant the oar in the mud down the river Fayit,]

[12] *pu sina teka jirima osara Saunatu pusina*
[12] sambil turun Saunatu tanam dayung
[12] Disembarking Saunatu plants the oar, [goes to plant the oar, Saunatu goes to plant the oar.]

[13] *teka irima osara Fayiti yaupu pusina teka jirima*
[13] di muara Fayit tanam dayung sambil minta matahari
[13] in the mouth of the Fayit plants the oar, besides asking for the sun. [Goes to plant the oar downriver the Fayit, goes to plant the oar.]

[14] *osara Fayiti yaupu pu sina teka jirima osara*
[14] muara Fayit yang indah baik sekali
[14] The beautiful mouth of the Fayit is the best. [He goes to plant the oar down the river Fayit, goes to plant the oar.]

[15] *yawi jara seja wimi timare Fayiti yawi jara seja wimi timare,*
[15] matahari cepat terbit sambil dia berteriak di perahu dia berteriak,
[15] The sun rises quickly while he screams in the canoe, he screams. [The sun comes down the river Fayit quickly.]

[16]*yawi jara seja wimi timare Fayiti yawi jara seja wimi timare,*

[16] matahari cepat terbit sambil dia berteriak di perahu dia berteriak,

[16] The sun rises quickly while he screams in the canoe, he screams. [First of all, come sun. First of all, come sun.]

[17] *yawi jara seja wimi timare Fayiti yawi jara seja wimi timare Fayiti tajara*

[17] matahari datang matahari Fayit cepat, matahari Fayit cepat

[17] The sun is coming, the sun Fayit is fast, the sun Fayit is fast, [The sun of river Fayit comes quickly. The sun of river Fayit comes quickly.]

[18] *seja wimi timare. Sawini pari sapena teka jirima*

[18] dayung tanam di lumpur sambil minta matahari

[18] plant the oar in the mud and ask for the sun at the same time. [The sun comes quickly. Sawini goes to plant the oar.]

[19] *osare jimi yaupu pari sapena teka irima osare*

[19] di muara suara burung juga bersuara

[19] At the estuary sounds the voice of the bird, [Downstream Fayit, go plant the oar and wait there.]

[20] *yasuru yara seja wimi timare jimi yaupu jasuru*

[20] matahari cepat datang di muara dia berteriak

[20] come sun quickly to the mouth of the river, he screams, [The sun comes up quickly. The sun of river Fayit comes quickly.]

[21] *jara seja wimi timare yasuru jara seja wimi timare*

[21] cepat matahari cepati terbit

[21] rise quickly sun, quickly. [The sun comes quickly. The sun comes quickly.]

[22] *yaka yasuru jara seja wimi timare.*

[22] aduh cepatkah matahari ini terbit.

[22] Oh! Is the sun rising quickly? [Sun, first of all come.]

Stanza 15

[1] *Sawinato mani umapu biva taita sumare pirii biva.*

[1] Sawinato pukul air laut dengan tangan

[1] Sawinato hits the water of the sea with the hand. [Sawinato, take your hand and beat the water at the sea, beat the water of the sea.]

[2] *Sawinato mani umapu biva taita sumare pirii biva.*

[2] Sawinato pukul air laut dengan tangan

[2] Sawinato hits the water of the sea with the hand. [Sawinato, take your hand and beat the water at the sea, beat the water of the sea.]

[3] *Taita somare Batia onamo bina basere*

[3] awan di bagian Batia harap baik

[3] The cloud in the region Batia is hopefully good. [Clouds over Batia (north of the Fayit - area south of the Fayit is called Safan) look calm.]

[4] *safani onamu bina basere batia onamu bina basere*

[4] awan di bagian Safan harap naik baik

[4] The cloud in the region Safan hopefully ascends well. [The clouds over Safan (south) look calm.]

[5] *Safani onamu bina basere Sawini mani uma*

[5] awan di bagian Safan harap baik Sawini pukul

[5] The cloud in the region Safan hopefully hits Sawini good. [The clouds over Safan look calm.]

[6] *pu biva taita sumare piri biva taita somare.*

[6] pukul air laut dengan dayung di atas air

[6] The water of the sea, hit the water with the oar, [Take your hand and beat the water of the sea. Take your hand and beat the water of the sea.]

[7] *Sawini mani umapu biva taita sumare piri biva*

[7] Sawini pukul air laut dengan tangan

[7] Sawini hits the water of the sea with the hand. [Sawini with your hand beat the water of the sea.]

[8] *taita sumare batia onamu bina basera Safani*

[8] sambil pukul dia minta air di bagian Safan

[8] While hitting, he asks the water in the region Safan. [When you beat the water of the sea, the clouds over Batia and the clouds over Safan look calm.]

[9] *onamu bina basere Sawini ifi umapu akami taita*

[9] Awan di atas cerah karena Sawini pukul air.

[9] The cloud above is bright because Sawini hits the water. [Sawini with your right hand beat the water of the sea.]

¹⁰ *sumare yo okamifa taita somare Sawini ifi umapu*

¹⁰ dia angkat tangan dan laut menjadi tenang

¹⁰ He lifts his hands and the sea became calm. [He begins to beat. Sawini with your right hand beat the water of the sea.]

¹¹ *okami taita sumare.*

¹¹ awan menjadi cerah.

¹¹ The cloud lightens up. [Beat the water of the sea.]

Stanza 16

¹ *Yoatiare yoatiare. Isamina pai timare*

¹ Di muara kali ada asap naik

¹ In the mouth of the river smoke ascends [Yoatiare (name of Yaptambor ancestor) makes smoke with a fire at the mouth of the river.]

² *Baini yaupu isa amina paitimare. Yoa tiare*

² muara kali Baini asap naik dari Yuator (= moyang kampung Tambor)

² In the mouth of the river Baini smoke ascends from Yuator (ancestor of the village Tambor) [Estuary of the Bayuni (river) smoke of fire comes out. Yoatiare.]

³ *isa amina pai timare Baini yaupu isa amina pai*

³ asap api di muara Baini siapa pasang

³ Smoke from the fire in estuary of the river Baini, who has made it? [The smoke of the fire begins to come out from the mouth of the river Bayun.]

⁴ *timare ya jina siri yanimare. Ya sina sia peja*

⁴ saya di tanah, anak-anak saya dalam tanah

⁴ I am on the earth, my children are under the earth. [The smoke begins to come out, oh children try to hear.]

⁵ *jaremare sinakufa sia peja jaremare*

⁵ saya betul-betul ada dalam tanah

⁵ I am really under the earth. [I just stay on the mud, I just stay on the mud.]

⁶ *ya jina siri jarimare du suna sia peja jaremare*

⁶ hai anak-anak saya ada di lumpur

⁶ Hey, my children in the swamp. [Oh children, I just stay on the mud, on the mud.]

[7] *sinaku fa sia peja jiaremare yocora.*

[7] Yuator mari naik ke atas, di dalam tanah tidak baik

[7] Yuator come up, it is not good under the earth. [Only sit on the mud, oh children, my name is Yocora (=Yoatiare).]

[8] *Isamina paitimare Baini yaupu isaaminapai*

[8] asap api ada naik di muara kali Baini

[8] Smoke from a fire ascends in the estuary of the river Baini. [Smoke of the fire is coming out from river Bayun. The smoke of the fire is coming out.]

[9] *timare yaituara isamini pari simare basar*

[9] sedang naik adalah asap api dari Yuator

[9] The ascending smoke of the fire is smoke of the fire of Yuator. [Smoke of fire is coming out, Yoatiare's smoke, smoke of the fire is coming out.]

[10] *yaupua yuraniami na pari sima ri yotuara*

[10] aduh saya punya muara kali bagus sambil goyang

[10] Oh my estuary of the river is very beautiful, as it moves. [Estuary of river Bayun comes out, the smoke of the fire belongs to Yoatiare.]

[11] *isa amina pari simare basar yaupu yurani*

[11] puntung api diangkat sambil goyang

[11] Glowing wood stump moves, [Smoke of the fire begins to come out of the mouth of river Basar (=Bayuni), smoke of the fire.]

[12] *amina pari simare duru sifa sia peja yaumimomare*

[12] asap api naik tapi saya di lumpur

[12] Smoke of the fire ascends, I am in the swamp. [The smoke of the fire begins to come out. I only sit on the mud.]

[13] *sapefa siape ja jaupi timare sape nakufa*

[13] engkau siapa yang datang karena saya di dalam tanah

[13] Who are you who comes because I am under the earth, [I sit only on the mud at the mouth of the river, I only sit on the mud,]

[14] *sia peja jaupi temare.*

[14] hanya asap naik.

[14] only ascending smoke. [only sit on the mud.]

Stanza 17

[1] *Basa mara para para ja wimisimare para para*
[1] Kilat sambar-sambar di malam hari [Kilat mulai sambar-sambar matahari capat naik kilat sambar-sambar (L.)]
[1] Lightning flashing in the night. [Lightning flashes and also the sun flashes.] [Lightning is beginning to hit the sun. Get in quickly, the flash is beginning to strike the sun. Get in quickly, the flashes are striking. (L.)]

[2] *jaumi simare para para ja jawimi timare*
[2] sambil kilat sambar-sambar sambil goyang [kilat sambar menanti saatnya (L.)]
[2] During the lightning it moves. [Lightning flashes down strongly and also the sun flashes down.] [The flashes are striking, are waiting for their time. (L.)]

[3] *basamara para para jajaumisimare basamara*
[3] Kilat sambar-sambar di malam hari [kilat sambar sambar kilat sambar sambar (L.)]
[3] Lightning is flashing in the night. [The lightning flashes down and starts, struck by lightning.] [The flashes are striking, the flashes are striking. (L.)]

[4] *para para ja ja umisimare bisa papara jawimisimare*
[4] sambil kilat sambar-sambar sambil goyang [menanti saat kilat sambar sambar menti (=menanti ?) saatnya]
[4] While the flash is striking, at the same time moves. [The lightning strikes over and over again.] [Waiting for the time that flashes strike, waiting for the time. (L.)]

[5] *bisa paprajawimitimare bisa parajaumitimare*
[5] malam hari kilat sambar-sambar [Menanti saat kilat sambar sambar (L.)]
[5] In the night the lightning flashes. [The lightning strikes in the early morning and is just flashing.] [Waiting for the moment when the flashes strike. (L.)]

[6] *basamara parapara jaumisimare basa mara*
[6] sambil kilat sambar-sambar sambil goyang [Menanti saat kilat sambar sambar (L.)]
[6] While the flash strikes, at the same time moves. [The lightning strikes and he waits for the lightning.] [Waiting for the moment when the flashes strike. (L.)]

[7] *paraimare para para ima umisimare*
[7] kilat sambar-sambar dan ia dalam tanah [sambar kilat mulai sambar sambar (L.)]
[7] The flash strikes and he in the earth. [The lightning begins to strike, strike and begins to strike.] [Strike, the flashes begin to strike. (L.)]

38

8 *beru paraimare para para jima umisimare*

8 kilat sambar-sambar, kilat sambar-sambar sepanjang malam. [Kilat sambar mulai
sambar sambar]

8 The flash strikes, the flash strikes the whole night through. [The lightning strikes
and strikes and begins to strike.] [The flashes strike, begin to strike. (L.)]

9 *beru para imare parapara jawimitimare*

9 kilat juga sambar-sambar, kilat juga sambar-sambar sampai pagi.

9 The lightning strikes, the lightning strikes until the morning. [The lightning begins
to strike, strikes and begins to strike.]

10 *beru apaparima umitimari baitua paparimaumitimare*

10 kilat samba mulai malam sampai pagi.

10 The lightning strikes in the evening until the morning. [The lightning begins to
strike and flashes up and down.]

11 *beru paparimaumi timare basu paparima umitimare*

11 barisan kilat menyambar ke seluruh tempat ini.

11 The series of flashes all strike this place. [The lightning opens its way to strike
and opens its way to strike.]

12 *beru paraimare para para jaumitimare*

12 kilat juga sambar-sambar, kilat juga sambar-sambar sampai pagi.

12 The lightning continues striking, the lightning continues striking until the
morning. [The lightning begins to strike and strike over and over again.]

13 *beru paraimare para para jaumitimare*

13 kilat sambar mulai malam sampai pagi.

13 The lightning strikes from evening till the morning. [The lightning begins to
strike and strikes over and over again.]

14 *basu paparima umitimare. Basua paparima*

14 barisan kilat turun dari atas ke tanah

14 The series of flashes comes from above down to the ground, [It opens and begins
to strike.]

15 *umitimare.*

15 dari tanah ke atas awan.

15 from the ground up to the clouds. [It begins to strike.]

Stanza 18

[1] *Uru fe bivaninima umiimare upi urua biva*
[1] Kilat juga sambar-sambar di atas air laut
[1] The flash also strikes over the sea. [The thunder puts its bottom into the water and finishes in the water.]

[2] *ninima umiimare uru biva ninimaumiimare*
[2] guntur juga turun ikut turun
[2] The thunder also descends. [The sound begins to come down to the water and its noise finishes in the water.]

[3] *piri uru biva ninima umiimare piri uru*
[3] laut engkau yang sudah biasa dengan guntur
[3] Sea which you have already been with the thunder several times. [The thunder at sea begins to come down. Thunder at sea begins to come down.]

[4] *biva ninima umiimare amunamna taua*
[4] air laut juga ikut goyang ikan laut pun takut
[4] The sea is raging, also the fish are afraid. [The sounds come down to the water and it sounds by itself.]

[5] *umitimare siri namnana tana umisimare*
[5] ikan bulanak pun takut karena guntur
[5] The *bulanak* fish is afraid because of the thunder. [The eyes of *siri* (name of a fish) make sounds.]

[6] *umutu namnana tana umitimare umutu*
[6] lagi pula ikan kuru besar panjang takut
[6] Besides of him, the large and long *kuru* fish is afraid. [Umutu (fish) begins to move and makes the sound. Umutu]

[7] *namnana tana umitimare siri namnana*
[7] ia mengambil ikan bulanak untuk dia
[7] He takes for himself the *bulanak* fish. [begins to move and *siri* begins to move.]

[8] *tana umitimare umutu namnana tana*
[8] juga ikan kuru besar dia ambil
[8] The large *kuru* fish he also takes. [Now he begins to make the sound. Umutu moves.]

40

[9] *umitimare uru biva ninima umiimare*

[9] ia adalah seorang pintar tombak ikan laut

[9] He is clever in spearing the sea fish. [The thunder begins to come down to the water.]

[10] *piri uru piri biva ninima umiimare*

[10] laut engkau punya laut

[10] Sea, you have the sea. [The thunder at sea begins to come down to water.]

[11] *urua biva ninima umiimare piri uru bibi*

[11] saya juga sudah dijadikan demikian

[11] I became so also. [The thunder begins to come down to the water. The thunder at sea comes down to the water,]

[12] *ninima umiimare uru biva ninima umiimare*

[12] sambil bicara begitu guntur jatuh ke laut

[12] While this conversation was being held the thunder came to the sea. [begins to make sounds down to the water.]

[13] *piriuru piri biva ninima umiimare*

[13] laut engkau punya laut

[13] Sea, you have the sea. [The thunder (*piri*) of the sea (*uru*) its sounds down to the water.]

[14] *biva ninima umiimare piri uru biva ninima*

[14] guntur turun dari daratan ke lautan

[14] The thunder moves from the land to the sea. [The water begins to move and the thunder of the sea comes down to the sea.]

[15] *umiimare*

[15] ambil pergi

[15] Take away. [The sounds come down.]

[16] *urua biva ninima umiimare umutu nam*

[16] guntur bunyi dan pergi ke laut

[16] The thunder roars and moves to the sea. [The thunder moves to the water and Umutu moves.]

[17] *nana tana umitimare umutu namnana*

[17] sambil jalan dan ambil ikan kuru

[17] While moving it takes the *kuru* fish. [It begins to sound. Umutu moves.]

18 tana umitimare akaya okami fa ni ni

18 ikan juga ikut pergi ke laut karena guntur

18 The fish moves also because of the thunder to the sea. [Now thunder begins to
sound and the sound is coming down to the water.]

19 maumiimare akaya okami ninima umiimare

19 bunyi yang pergi ke laut adalah guntur

19 The noise that moves into the sea is the thunder. [The sounds come down to the
water and it comes down to the water.]

20 yoa akaya okami ninima umiimare amu

20 ikan kakap juga ikut pergi ke laut

20 The *kakap* fish also joins moving to the sea. [The thunder of the sea comes down
to the sea, begins to sound and to come down.]

21 nantana pa tana umitimare isu namtani tana

21 ikan yang pergi semua adalah kakap, kuru, bulanak

21 All fish who move are *kakap, kuru, bulanak.* [Isu (= Umutu) forces himself to
make a movement and begins to move,]

22 umitimare sirinamtani pa tana umitimare

22 yang ikut bawa ikan-ikan adalah guntur

22 What the fish take with themselves is the thunder. [begins to sound. *Siri* (fish)
moves to create sounds.]

23 yani namtani pa tana umitimare akaya okami

23 bunyi saja yang pergi adalah bunyi guntur

23 The noise which only moves is that of the thunder. [*Jani* (fish) begins to move,
the thunder in the water.]

24 ninima umiimare yoa aka ya okamifa

24 laut punya Guntur bunyinya keras

24 The thunder of the sea roars loudly. [The sounds begin to come down, the thunder
of the sea begins to come down to the water.]

25 ninima umiimare.

25 serentak bunyi guntur laut.

25 Suddenly the thunder of the sea roars. [The sounds come down.]

42

Stanza 19

[1] *Saunatu yoapu ameini mu mari basini tamen*
[1] Saunatu berubah jadi ikan belut
[1] Saunatu turnes into an eel. [Saunatu is perspiring and makes himself like an eel.]

[2] *pa yaura ainimare pa yaura ainimare*
[2] sambil jalan ke arah laut, sambil jalan ke arah laut
[2] While walking into the direction of the sea, while his walk towards the sea, [He already turned into an eel, already turned into an eel.]

[3] *Saunatu pa yaura ainimare basini tameni paya*
[3] Saunatu menjelma jadi belut
[3] Saunatu turnes into an eel. [Saunatu already turned into an eel, already turned into an eel.]

[4] *ura ainimare pa yaura ainimare yaupu*
[4] menuju ke muara arah laut
[4] To the estuary in the direction of the sea. [It's happened already, it's already happened.]

[5] *ma tutufia ainimare namu yapuna pa*
[5] karena banyaknya keringat ia menjelma
[5] He who sweated so strongly transforms himself. [He already walked away full of sweat. He already walked away full of sweat.]

[6] *tutufa ainimare yaupuna tutufima ainimare*
[6] ke muara kali Baini dan jadi di situ
[6] To the estuary of the river Baini and there it happened. [Full of sweat he goes away. Full of sweat he goes away.]

[7] *yaupuma tutufima ainimare*
[7] sambil diantar dengan tangan
[7] While he was lead by the hand, [While perspiring he walks away.]

[8] *Saunatu pu aya ini mumari basini tameni*
[8] Saunatu jalan terus karena telah jadi belut.
[8] Saunatu moves on because he turned into an eel. [Saunatu begins to go away like an eel.]

[9] *pa yaura ainimare payaura a yi nimare*

[9] dia pergi dan akan jadi belut di sana

[9] He goes and there turns into an eel. [He walks away, he walks away.]

[10] *Sawini titi pari aya ini mu mari ajainimu*

[10] Sawini dayung di pinggir atas laut

[10] Sawini rows on the edge of the sea. [Sawini is full of sweat, full of sweat he
   walks away.]

[11] *mari payaura ainimare Sawini tuaruta*

[11] ada Sawini menjadi belut tanah

[11] There is Sawini, who turned into an earth eel, [He walks away. He walks away.
   Sawini turned into an eel.]

[12] *meni payaura ainimare*

[12] maka terjadi di situ

[12] that happened there. [He already turned into an eel and then walks away.]

[13] *tuaru tamene nimi pa yaura ainimare*

[13] dia menjelma menjadi belut [jadi belut baru jalan jalan. (L.)]

[13] He changes into an eel. [He turned into an eel and then walked and walked.]
   [transformed into an eel, begins to move away. (L.)]

[14] *tuaru tamene nimi pa yaura ainimare*

[14] ada juga menjelma menjadi belut rawa [jadi belut baru jalan jalan. (L.)]

[14] There is also the one who turned into a swamp eel. [He turned into an eel and
   then walked and walked.] [transformed into an eel, begins to move on. (L.)]

[15] *Sawini tuar tamene nimi pa yaura ainimare*

[15] Sawini menjelma menjadi belut [Sawini jadi belut baru jalan. (L.)]

[15] Sawini changes into an eel. [Sawini turns into an eel, then walks.] [Sawini turned
   into an eel, begins to move on. (L.)]

[16] *tuaru tamenenimi pa yaura ainimare*

[16] ada juga menjelma menjadi belut rawa [jadi belut baru jalan. (L.)]

[16] There is also the one who changed into a swamp eel. [He turned into an eel and
   then walked and walked.] [Turned into an eel, begins to move on. (L.)]

[17] *biri pitinianimi titiva ainimare*

[17] air seperti warna bulu burung Urip

[17] The water is like the colour of the feather of the *urip* bird. [His skin like *biri*
   (fish). The sweat drops come out of his body and he walks.]

[18] *tuaru tamene nimi pa tutu fima ainimare*
[18] sambil jalan dia tarik pergi [jadi belut baru jalan jalan. (L.)]
[18] While walking he moves away, [Turns into an eel and then walks and walks.]
[transformed into an eel he moves away. (L.)]

[19] *tuaru tamene nima pa tutu fima ainimare*
[19] menjelma jadi belut [jadi belut baru jalan jalan. (L.)]
[19] changes to an eel. [Turns into an eel and then walks and walks.] [Turned into an
eel, begins to move away. (L.)]

[20] *tutu fima ainimare tuaru tamene nimi pa*
[20] sambil jalan dia tarik pergi [Mandi keringat seperti belut. (L.)]
[20] While walking he moves away, [Lots of sweat came out like an eel.] [He sweats
strongly just like an eel. (L.)]

[21] *tutu fima ainimare pa yau re ainimare*
[21] tarik sambil jalan dan tarik [Mandi keringat suda jadi mau jalan (L.)]
[21] moves, while walking and moves [Lots of sweat, he became like an eel and
walks.] [He sweats and has become, wants to move on. (L.)]

[22] *Dua doratia piri du duru yarkinase*
[22] ikan lumba-lumba dan saya [Dua saya punya perut saya punya perut (L.)]
[22] the dolphin and I. [Dua (fish), you are my stomach. Dua, you are my stomach.]
[Dua, I have belly, I have belly. (L.)]

[23] *Dua duru kena serame piri Dua duruakena*
[23] ikan lumba-lumba ada mau dengan saya [Dua ini saya dua engkau saya punya
perut (L.)]
[23] The dolphin feels with me, [Dua, this is me. Dua, you are my stomach.] [This
Dua I am, Dua are you, I have belly. (L.)]

[24] *se piri Dua ara awajafa sarama sumare*
[24] ikan lumba-lumba adalah bapa saya [Dua di laut engkau adalah saya punya bapa (L.)]
[24] the dolphin is my father. [Dua in the sea, you are my father.] [Dua in the sea, you
are my dad. (L.)]

[25] *Saunatu piri Du ara usi sarama sumare*
[25] Saunatu beri nama ikan lumba-lumba adalah mamanya [Saunatu kasi nama Du di
laut sama mama punya nama (L.)]
[25] Saunatu gives the dolphin name is his mother. [In the sea Saunatu gives his
mothers name to the Dua.] [Saunatu gives the name Du in the sea, the name of
the mother. (L.)]

²⁶ *Sawini yoa supuru ara awayafa sarama*

²⁶ Sawini ikan lumba-lumba adalah orang tuanya [Sawini kasih nama Du di laut
  sama mama punya nama (L.)]

²⁶ Sawini, the dolphin is his parents. [Sawini gives his mother's name to the Dua in
  the sea.] [Sawini gives the name Du in the sea, the name of the mother. (L.)]

²⁷ *sumare Sawini yoa supuru ara awaya*

²⁷ Sawini hanyut di atas air laut seperti kayu hanyut [Sawini kasih nama Dua di laut
  sama mama punya nama. (L.)]

²⁷ Sawini swims on the sea like driftwood. [Sawini gives his mother's name to the Dua
  in the sea,] [Sawini gives the name Dua in the sea, the name of the mother. (L.)]

²⁸ *sarama sumare ara awajafa sarama*

²⁸ kayu hanyut itu juga dikasih nama orangtua [Kasih nama bapa kasih mama (L.)]

²⁸ The driftwood was given the name of the parents. [gives his father's name to the
  Dua, gives the name.] [Gives the name dad, gives mum, (L.)]

²⁹ *sumare supuru ara awaja fa rama sumare*

²⁹ kayu hanyut di laut dia beri nama tete (kakek) [kasih nama engkau adalah saya
  punya bapa (L.)]

²⁹ The timber floats into the sea, he gives the name grandfather. [Giving name to
  you, you are my father.] [give you name, is my father. (L.)]

³⁰ *supuru duru awaja fa kenasereme*

³⁰ kayu hanyut di laut dia beri nama nenek [Supuru engkau adalah saya punya bapa (L.)]

³⁰ The timber floats into the sea, he gives the name grandmother. [Supuru, you are
  my father.] [Supuru, you are my dad. (L.)]

³¹ *Sawini yua supuru ara awajafa sarama*

³¹ Sawini beri nama kayu hanyut di laut adalah ikan busuk [Sawini kasih nama
  Supuru di laut dengan nama bapanya (L.)]

³¹ Sawini gives the timber that was drifted into the sea the name smelling fish.
  [Sawini gives his fathers name to the Supuru (left name of Dua),] [gives the
  name Supuru in the sea, the name of his father, (L.)]

³² *sumare Sawini yoa supuru ara awajafa*

³² Sawini punya nenek sambil goyang [kasih nama Sawini kasih nama Supuru di
  laut dengan nama bapa (L.)]

³² Sawini has grandmother, while dancing. [giving name. Sawini gives his father's
  name to the Supuru.] [gives the name. Sawini gives the name Supuru in the sea,
  his father's name, (L.)]

[33] *sara ma sumare supuru duru awajafa kena*
[33] engkau saya punya tete [kasih nama Supuru engkau adalah saya punya bapa (L.)]
[33] You are my grandfather. [Giving the name Supuru, you are my father.] [gives the
   name Supuru. You are my dad. (L.)]

[34] *serame oyua supuru duru awajafa kenaserame*
[34] Sawini punya nenek sambil goyang [Engkau yang tinggal Supuru engkau adalah
   saya punya bapa. (L.)]
[34] Sawini has grandmother, while dancing. [I know you, you must be Supuru and
   you are my father.] [You Supuru who stays. You are my dad (L.)]

[35] *ara awajafa kena serame supuru duru awajafa*
[35] engkau saya punya tete [saya punya bapa engkau yang tinggal adalah saya punya
   bapa (L.)]
[35] You are my grandfather. [You are there and must be Supuru and you are my
   father.] [My father are you who you stay are my father. (L.)]

[36] *kena serame.*
[36] betul engkau yang tinggal. [Engkau yang tinggal. (L.)]
[36] That's it, you stay. [You are there.] [You who you stay. (L.)]

Stanza 20

[1] *Sawini wi ipiri fua pata pima umi rimare*
[1] Anyaman rambut Sawini diayun angin [Sawini punya rambut angin yang tarik.
   (L.)]
[1] The braid of Sawini is blown away by the wind, [Sawini, your hair, the wind pulls
   it,] [The hair of Sawini is being pulled by the wind. (L)]

[2] *Pisi ipi fua pata pima umi kimare*
[2] dari angin laut dari timur [Angin Pisi yang tarik]
[2] by the sea's east wind. [The wind of Pisi (river) pulls it.] [The wind of Pisi, it
   pulls. (L.)]

[3] *Sawini wiipiri fua pata pima umi kimare*
[3] anyaman rambut Sawini ditiup angin dari laut [Sawini punya rambut angin Pisi
   yang tarik (L.)]
[3] The braid of Sawini is blown by the wind of the sea. [Sawini's hair, the wind of
   the river Wi (=Pisi) pulls it.] [The hair of Sawini is pulled by the wind of Pisi.
   (L)]

⁴ *wiipiri fua pata pima umi kimare Pisi fua pata pime*
⁴ ujung rambutnya sampai ke darat [Punya rambut angin Pisi yang tarik (L.)]
⁴ His hair-end reaches the land. [The wind of Pisi pulls the hair.] [Your hair is
     pulled by the wind of Pisi. (L)]

⁵ *umikimare foa yafu temare foa yafu temare*
⁵ ujung rambutnya sampai pada muara kali [mulai jalan mulai jalan pergi lingkar
     (L.)]
⁵ His hair-ends reach the estuary of the river. [The wind begins to go, the wind
     begins to circle,] [Begins to move on, begins to move on, then revolves in a
     circle. (L.)]

⁶ *Yi bapanifa foa yafu temare fua yafu temarea*
⁶ ujung rambutnya terlipat di batang cemara [per lingkar di batang pohon Ji pergi
     lingkar (L.)]
⁶ The ends of his hair are entangled around the tree trunk of the casuarina tree.
     [going to circle at the tree trunk of the *yi*, going to circle.] [Entangled in the *ji*
     tree, moves on, entangles itself. (L.)]

⁷ *fua yafu temare jibapanifa foa yafu temare*
⁷ angin engkau sungguh baik dan nikmat [mulai lingkar di batang pohon ji pergi
     lingkar (L.)]
⁷ Wind, you are very good and pleasant. [Begins to circle around the tree trunk of
     the *yi*, going to circle.] [Begins to entangle around the *ji* tree, moves on and
     entangles itself. (L.)]

⁸ *foa yafu temare foa yafu temare jibapanifa foa*
⁸ angin engkau sungguh baik dan nikmat [pergi lingkar pergi lingkar di batang ji
     (L.)]
⁸ Wind, you are very good and pleasant. [going to circle, going to circle around
     the tree trunk of the *yi*.] [Moves away and entangles itself, moves away and
     entangles itself around the tree trunk of the *ji*. (L.)]

⁹ *yafu temere foa yafutemarea fua yafu*
⁹ angin engkau bagaikan burung urip [pergi lingkar pergi lingkar (L.)]
⁹ You are like the *urip* bird. [going to circle, going to circle.] [Moves away and
     entangles itself, moves away and entangles itself. (L.)]

[10] *temare jibapanifa foa yafu temare Saunatu wi ipiri*

[10] rambut Saunatu sudah lipat di batang pohon cemara [pergi lingka(r) di batang ji pergi lingkar Saunatu punya rambut. (L.)]

[10] The hair of Saunatu already on the tree trunk of the casuarina tree. [Going to circle at the tree trunk of the *yi*, going to circle at the hair of Saunatu.] [Moves away and entangles itself in the tree trunk of the *ji*, moves away and the hair of Saunatu entangles itself. (L.)]

[11] *fua pata pima umi kimare Pisi ipi fua pata*

[11] angin di laut yang tiup ke darat [angin yang tiup angin Pisi yang tiup. (L.)]

[11] The wind in the sea, which blows towards the land. [The wind that blows is the wind of the river Pisi, that's blowing.] [The wind blows, the wind from Pisi blows. (L.)]

[12] *pima umi kimore Sawini somenipiri isisia pata*

[12] ujung rambut Sawini ditiup angin laut [Mau tiup Sawini engkau punya angin Pisi mau tiup (L.)]

[12] The hair-ends of Sawini are blown away by the sea wind. [The wind that blows Sawini's hair is the wind of Pisi.] [Wants to blow Sawini. Your wind Pisi wants to blow, (L)]

[13] *pima umi kimare Sefara bapan isisi pata pima umikimare*

[13] angin yang kencang membuat putus rambut [mau tiup di batang serabapan angin mau tiup. (L.)]

[13] The strong wind makes the hair broken. [The wind blows at the tree trunk of the *sefarabapan* tree, the wind blows.] [Wants to blow on the tree trunk of the *serabapan* tree. The wind wants to blow. (L.)]

[14] *Sawini someipiri isisi pata pima umikimare*

[14] Sawini punya rambut dipotong oleh angin [Sawini engkau punya ramput angin mau tiup. (L.)]

[14] The hair of Sawini was cut by the wind, [Sawini, your hair the wind likes to blow.] [Sawini, the wind wants to blow your hair. (L.)]

[15] *se ipiri isisipata pima umikimare se yafutema rea*

[15] pergi dan lipat di batang pohon [Angin mau tiup mau tiup pergi mau pergi lingkar]

[15] move and entangle around the tree trunk, [The wind wants to blow, go, wants to blow, wants to circle,] [The wind wants to blow, wants to blow away, wants to move on and entangle itself. (L.)]

¹⁶ *se bapanifa seyafutemare*

¹⁶ lipat di batang pohon cemara [mau peru lingkar di batang sebapani (L.)]

¹⁶ entangle around the tree trunk of the casuarina tree. [wants to circle at the tree trunk of the *sebapani* tree,] [Wants to move on and entangle itself around the tree trunk of the *sebapani* tree. (L.)]

¹⁷ *auni bapanifa teka yafu temare auni-bapanifa teka yafu*

¹⁷ batang pohon cemara penuh dengan rambut anyaman [mau pergi lingkar di batang pohon Auni Bapani (L.)]

¹⁷ The tree trunk of the casuarina tree is full of the plaited hair, [wants to circle at the tree trunk of the *aunibapanifa* tree,] [Wants to move on and entangle itself around the tree trunk of the *auni-bapani* tree. (L.)]

¹⁸ *temare.*

¹⁸ penuh anyaman rambut. [pergi lingkar. (L.)]

¹⁸ full of plaited hair. [going to circle.] [moves on and entangles itself. (L.)]

Stanza 21

¹ *Sawinatu turu mana yape wawya ainimare*

¹ Sawinatu tidak pakai bulu burung kakatua (=turu)[Sawinatu jalan dengan bulu kuning kakatua yang bergoyang-goyang. (P.)] [Sawinatu pake bulu Yakob mau paka jalan. (L.)]

¹ Sawinatu doesn't wear the feather of the parrot. [Sawinatu goes with a yellow cockatoo feather which moves to and fro. (P)] [Sawinatu wears cockatoo feathers during the walking.] [Sawinatu wears the feather Jacob, wants to go wearing. (L.)]

² *tiwauta barabaraya ainire Saunatu turumana*

² di tengah perahu sambil berkilauan Saunatu tidak pakai [Di tengah perahu Saunatu jalan dengan bulu dengan bulu kuning kakatua yang berkilau-kilauan. (P.)] [di tenga perahu sambar jalan Saunatu punya bulu Yakob (L.)]

² In the middle of the canoe, during the glittering Saunatu doesn't wear it. [In the middle of the canoe Saunatu rows with a yellow cockatoo feather which glitters. (P.)] [In the middle of the canoe on which Saunatu stands the feathers of the cockatoo glitter.] [In the middle of the canoe strikes, goes the feather Jacob of Saunatu. (L.)]

³ *tiwautafa barabaraya ainimare tiwautafa*

³ bulu burung kakatua berkilauan. Ditengah perahu berkilauan [Di tengah perahu jalan berkilau-kilau (P.)] [Di tenga perahu sambar sambar baru jalan di tenga perahu (L.)]

³ The feather of the cockatoo is glittering. In the middle of the canoe it is flashing. [In the middle of the canoe rows, it glitters (P.)] [In the middle of the canoe flashing, want to go in the middle of the canoe.] [In the middle of the canoe it strikes, begins to row in the middle of the canoe. (L.)]

⁴ *bara bara ya ainimare waita ayera bare Tamatapis*

⁴ dia pergi langsung ke Yai (=rumah adat) Tamutapis [Di tengah perahu jalan dengan berkilau merencanakan perang (P.)]

⁴ He goes straight to the *yai* (= men's or ritual house) Tamutapis. [In the middle of the canoe he rows in the middle of the canoe, it glitters, he plans a war, he plans a war (P.)] [Flashing, want to make war.]

⁵ *waitia a ye era bari dia duru waitia*

⁵ bapa saya mau lempar sekarang [Perang dengan Tamatapis. Bapa, saya pergi berperang (P.)]

⁵ My father wanted to throw now. [War with Tamatapis. Dad, I make war (P.)] [Makes war against Tamutapis (place for women, who died at a birth).]

⁶ *ayeera bare yiwi waitia ayera bari Tamatapis*

⁶ Tamutapis saya mau lempar ini [mau pergi perang dengan Tamatapis (L.)] [Pergi berperang dengan Yiwi dan Tamatapis. (P.)]

⁶ Tamutapis I wanted to throw this. [He wants to make war. I make the war.] [Want to make war with Tamatapis. (L.)] [Saunatu makes war with Yiwi and Tamatapis. (P.)]

⁷ *waitia ayaera bare Saunatu turu mana barabaraya*

⁷ dalam perahu bulu burung Saunatu berkilauan [mau pergi perang Saunatu pake bulu kakatua jalan sambar sambar (L.)] [Saunatu pergi berperang dan jalan dengan bulu kuning kakatua yang berkilauan. (P)]

⁷ In the canoe the bird's feather of Saunatu glitters, [Wants to make war, Saunatu wears a cockatoo feather now striking (L.)] [Saunatu makes war and rows with a yellow cockatoo feather which glitters (P.)]

[8] *ainimare tiwautafa barabaraya ainimare*

[8] dalam perahu bulu burung kakatua berkilauan [jalan di tenga perahu jalan sambar-
sambar. (L.)] [Di tengah perahu ia jalan dengan berkilauan (P.)]

[8] in the canoe the feather of a cockatoo is glittering. [In the middle of the canoe he
rows, it glitters (P.)] [Rows in the middle of the canoe, rows striking, (L.)]

[9] *barabaraya ainibapi ti waufafa barabaraya*

[9] di depan perahu dia berkilauan seperti bulu burung kakatua [sambar sambar
jalan di tenga perahu jalan sambar sambar (L.)] [Dengan berkilauan ia jalan di
tengah perahu, ia jalan dengan berkilauan. (P.)]

[9] In front of the canoe it glitters just like the feather of the cockatoo. [striking rows
in the middle of the canoe, rows striking. (L.)] [Glittering he rows in the middle
of the canoe, he rows flashing (P.)]

[10] *ainimare barabaraya ainimare ti wautafa*

[10] pergi dengan perahu tapi berkilauan [jalan sambar di tenga perahu (L.)] [Dengan
berkilauan ia jalan di tengah perahu (P.)]

[10] He rides with the canoe but glitters, [Rides striking in the middle of the canoe,
(L.)] [Flashing he rows in the middle of the canoe (P.)]

[11] *barbaraya ainimare*

[11] tengah perahu berkilauan [sambar sambar jalan (L.)] [Dengan berkilauan ia jalan.
(P.)]

[11] the middle of the canoe. [rows striking. (L.)] [Flashing he rows. (P.)]

[12] *Sawini turu mana barabaraya ainimare*

[12] Sawini pakai bulu burung kakatua yang berkilauan [Sawini punya bulu kakatua
jalan sambar sambar (L.)] [Sawini jalan dengan bulu kuning kakatua yang
berkilau-kilauan. (P.)]

[12] Sawini wears the glittering feather of the cockatoo, [Sawini, cockatoo feather
rows striking. (L.)] [Sawini rows with the yellow cockatoo feather which
glitters. (P.)]

[13] *yai wautafa barabaraya ainimare*

[13] di tengah perahu berkilauan [salan sambar sambar di tenga perahu (L.)] [Di
tengah perahu dengan berkilauan ia jalan. (P.)]

[13] in the middle of the canoe it glitters. [Rows striking in the middle of the canoe,
(L.)] [In the middle of the canoe he rows flashing. (P.)]

[14] *wautafa barabaraya ainimare. Awaja duru*

[14] di tengah perahu berkilauan [di tenga perahu jalan sambar sambar baru jalan (L.)] [Di tengah perahu dengan berkilauan ia jalan. (P.)]

[14] In the middle of the canoe it glitters, [In the middle of the canoe, he rows striking, begins to row. (L.)] [In the middle of the canoe he rows flashing. (P.)]

[15] *namtana ayaera baye Jiapisi namtana*

[15] sambil dayung perahu [mau pergi perang perempuan-perempuan jia Pisi (L.)] [Bapa, saya pergi berperang melawan Yiapisi (=Tamatapis), perang. (P.)]

[15] while rowing the canoe. [Wants to wage war against the women Yiapisi. (L.)] [Dad, I wage war against Yiapisi (= Tamatapis), in the battle. (P.)]

[16] *ayeera bare awaya duru namtana aye*

[16] aduh saya punya badan, aduh bapa yo [mau pergi perang bapa saya mau pergi perang (L.)] [Bapa, saya pergi berperang melawan Yiapisi (P.)]

[16] Oh, my body, Oh, father, come, [Want to wage war, dad, I want to wage war. (L.)] [Dad, I wage war against Yiapisi (P.)]

[17] *era bare Jiapisi namtani aye era bare*

[17] aduh saya punya badan, aduh mama yo [mau pergi perang dengan perempuan jia Pisi (L.)] [Pergi berperang. (P.)]

[17] Oh, my body, Oh, mother, come. [Want to wage war against the woman Jiapisi. (L.)] [Wage war. (P.)]

[18] *namtana ayeera bare Jia pisi (Jia pis=roh) namtana aye*

[18] saya mau pergi ke tempat perempuan-perempuan roh [mau pergi perang dengan perempuan Jia Pisi (L.)] [Pergi berperang melawan Yiapisi, pergi berperang. (P.)]

[18] I want to go to the place of the spirits of women. [Want to wage war against the woman Jiapisi. (L.)] [Wage war against Jiapisi, go into the battle (P.)]

[19] *era bare Sauwini namtana ayeera bare*

[19] Sauwini mau makan di sana, ada sagu, ikan [mau perang Sawini mau pergi perang (L.)] [Sauwini pergi berperang melawan Yiwi (P.)]

[19] Sauwini wants to eat there, there is sago, fish, [Wants to wage war, Sawini wants to wage war. (L.)] [Sauwini goes into the battle against Yiwi (P.)]

[20] *jiwi namtana ayeera bare barabaraja*

[20] saya mau pergi dan harus makan di sana [mau pergi perang mau pergi perang (L.)] [Pergi berperang dengan berkilau, ia jalan. (P.)]

[20] I want to go there and have to eat there. [Want to make war, want to make war. (L.)] [Goes into the battle, flashing, he goes. (P.)]

[21] *ainimare Sawini witau barabaraya ainimara*

[21] di kepala Sawini ada bulu burung berkilauan [mau jalan Sawini di tenga perahu jalan
   sambar sambar (L.)] [Sawini jalan dengan kepala yang berkilau-kilauan. (P.)]

[21] On the head of Sawini there is a flashing bird's feather. [Wants to row, Sawini in the
   middle of the canoe rows striking. (L.)] [Sawini goes with flashing head. (P.)]

[22] *bara ya ainimare yai wautafa barabaraya*

[22] sambil dayung di tengah perahu berkilauan [sambar sambar jalan di tenga
   perahu sambar sambar (L.)] [Jalan dengan berkilauan di tengah perahu, dengan
   berkilauan ia jalan. (P.)]

[22] While rowing the canoe it glitters. [Striking rows in the middle of the canoe,
   striking. (L.)] [He rows with flashing in the middle of the canoe. Glittering he
   rows (P.)]

[23] *ainimare barabaraya ainimare. Yai*

[23] sedang berkilauan di kepala [jalan sambar sambar. Sambar sambar baru jalan
   (L.)] [Dengan berkilauan ia jalan. (P.)]

[23] It just glitters on the head, [Rows striking, begins to row striking. (L.)] [Glittering
   he rows. (P.)]

[24] *wautafa barabaraya ainimare.*

[24] di tengah-tengah juga berkilauan di kepala. [di tenga perahu jalan sambar sambar
   (L.)] [Di tengah perahu dengan berkilauan ia jalan. (P.)]

[24] in the middle it also glitters on the head. [In the middle of the canoe rows
   striking. (L.)] [In the middle of the canoe he rows flashing. (P.)]

Stanza 22

[1] *Usuru (usuru=ikan pari) biijirai ya serame ya bi ijiraiifa*

[1] Ikan pari senang karena air laut baik [Ikan pari engkau dalam air dalam air (L.)]
   [Ikan pari kipas-kipas air, kipas-kipas air (P.)]

[1] Ray is happy because of the good sea. [Ray, you are in the water, you are in the
   water. (L.)] [Ray (Usuru) hits the water with the fins, hits the water. (P.)]

[2] *Ya serame usuru bijirai ifa ya serame*

[2] karena laut teduh ia jalan baik [dalam air. Ikan pari engkau dalam air. (L.)] [Ikan
   pari kipas-kipas air. (P.)]

[2] Because the sea is calm he swims well. [In the water. Ray you are in the water.
   (L.)] [Ray hits the water. (P.)]

[3] *piri usuru bisinibi jiraifa ya serame*

[3] ikan pari laut senang air laut. [Pari laut engkau senang diatas pasir laut.(L.)] [Piri
(laut) ikan pari kipas-kipas air di pinggir pasir di laut (bisinibi) (P.)]

[3] Ray of the sea is happy because of the sea. [Ray of the sea, you are happy on the
sand-beach of the sea. (L.)] [*Piri* (sea) ray hits the water in the sea close to the
coast. (P.)]

[4] *tutuma tutuma witinimare bifa tutuma*

[4] sayapnya merayap di atas permukaan laut [jalan kipas kipas dalam air (L.)]
[Dengan riak-riak air gelombang (tutuma) ia jalan dengan riak air. (P.)]

[4] Its wings float on the sea surface. [It swims with the fins in the water. (L.)] [With
tumult in water (*tutuma* = turn up the water), waves, swims turning up the water.
(P.)]

[5] *tutuma witi nimare birima tutuma tutuma*

[5] sayapnya merayap di atas permukaan laut [kipas kipas diatas jalan kipas kipas
(L.)] [Dengan membuat riak air (tutuma) ia jalan dengan riak air. (P.)]

[5] Its wings float on the sea surface. [Above it moves its fins and swims moving the fins.
(L.)] [With the produced tumult in the water he swims with turned up water. (P.)]

[6] *witimare tutuma tutuma witinimare*

[6] pari laut senang air laut [jalan kipas kipas diatas air. (L.)] [Dengan membuat riak
air membuat riak air (tutuma) ia jalan tutuma, tutuma. (P.)]

[6] Ray is happy because of the sea. [Swims moving the fins on the surface of the
water. (L.)] [With the produced tumult in the water, with the produced tumult in
the water he swims turning up the water, turning up the water. (P.)]

[7] *birima tutuma tutuma witinimare*

[7] tidak terbang di atas tapi lajunya seperti di atas [Jalan sambil kipas kipas diatas
permukaan air. (L.)] [Ia jalan dengan tutuma, dengan tutuma. (P.)]

[7] It doesn't fly over it, but its speed is like above. [Swims and at the same time
moves the fins on the surface of the water. (L.)] [He swims and turns up the
water, and turns up the water. (P.)]

[8] *birima tutuma tutuma witinimare birima*

[8] sambil jalan sambil sayapnya main [Sambil kipas air baru jalan. (L.)] [Ia jalan
dengan tutuma, tutuma. (P.)]

[8] Walking his wing plays. [Hits the water at the same time and swims. (L.)] [He
swims and turns up the water, and turns up the water. (P.)]

⁹ *tutuma tutuma witinimare usuru bijirai*

⁹ Ia bisa begitu karena laut teduh [Jalan kipas ikan pari diatas air (L.)] [ia jalan
dengan tutuma, tutuma. Usuru kipas-kipas air. (P.)]

⁹ He can (do) something like this, because the sea is calm. [Swims hitting, the ray
on the surface of the water. (L.)] [He swims and turns up the water, turns up the
water. Usuru hits the water. (P.)]

¹⁰ *ifa yaserame piri usuru bi jirajifa ya*

¹⁰ dia senang karena air laut cocok dia [engkau di air senang di dalam air. (L.)] [Pari
laut kipas-kipas air (P.)]

¹⁰ He is happy because the sea suits him. [You are in the water, like to be in the
water. (L.)] [Ray hits the water. (P.)]

¹¹ *serame tamutu ukami jirajifa yaserame*

¹¹ engkau pergi juga ke tempat yang saya jalan [Engkau dalam air engkau dalam air.
(L.)] [Usuru (=Tamutu) kipas-kipas air. (P.)]

¹¹ You also go to the place where I go. [You are in the water, you are in the water.
(L.)] [Tamutu (left name of the ray Usuru is Yua Tamutu) hits the water. (P.)]

¹² *yua tamutu seri ukami jirajifa yaserame*

¹² laut punya ikan pari senang laut. [Ikan pari di laut engkau senang dalam air (L.)]
[Pari laut kipas-kipas air (P.)]

¹² Ray (Yua Tumutu) is happy because of the sea. [Ray of the sea, you enjoy being
in the water. (L.)] [Ray hits the water. (P.)]

¹³ *tutuma tutuma witinimare yoa okamima*

¹³ sambil jalan sambil sayapnya main [jalan kipas kipas air air di laut (L.)] [ia jalan
dengan membuat riak air, yua ukami (=sea water). (P.)]

¹³ Walking its wing joins the game. [He swims and hits the water, the seawater, (L.)]
[He swims and turns up the water at the same time, seawater. (P.)]

¹⁴ *tutuma tutuma witinimare*

¹⁴ air laut dari itu dia senang [jalan kipas jalan kipas sambil jalan. (L.)] [Dengan
membuat riak-riak air ia pergi. (P.)]

¹⁴ The sea of that what makes him happy. [swims hitting, swims hitting, swims at
the same time. (L.)] [He swims with the turned up water. (P.)]

[15] *yoa okamima tutuma tutuma witinimare.*

[15] air laut dari itu dia senang. [jalan kipas ekor di atas air laut jalan. (L.)] [Ia jalan dengan membuat riak-riak air di air laut. (P.)]

[15] The sea of that what makes him happy. [He swims and moves the tail to and fro on the surface of the sea, swims. (L.)] [He swims and turns up the seawater at the same time. (P.)]

Stanza 23

[1] *Taiyuruwiata puya tama orani tipu ya tama oranie*

[1] Taiyuruwiata tolong dayung perahu saya.

[1] Taiyuruwiata helps me row the boat.

[2] *sayi ata puya tama rani puya ata usi iata namu*

[2] Sayiara tolong dayung gaya dayung daun kayu badan.

[2] Sayiara helps me rowing. The form of the oar wood-leaf body.

[3] *jie ainimare usi iayato na muji etemare*

[3] Ciptaan daun kayu senang sekali indahnya.

[3] The image wood-leaf is proud of its beauty.

[4] *bisini tuni usi iyi ayato namu ji etemare*

[4] Pasir atas pohon semua bagus indah sekali.

[4] The sand on the tree is all good, very beautiful.

[5] *usiulayato na muji etemare bisini tuni*

[5] Segala daun kayu indah sekali yang diatas fasir.

[5] Every wood-leaf is very beautiful on the sand.

[6] *usiiayato namuji itimare namuji itimare*

[6] Gayanya baik sekali semua gayanya baik sekali.

[6] Its form is very beautiful, all its form is very beautiful.

[7] *usiiayato namuji itimare puja tamure*

[7] Senang sekali segala daun sambil dayung.

[7] Very enjoying is every leaf when rowing.

[8] *Tipu ja tamurie Taiyuruwiata puja tamure*

[8] Perahu di dayung oleh Tayuruwiata.

[8] The canoe is being rowed by Tayuruwiata.

[9] *Tipu ja tamure puja tamure tipuja tamure*
[9] Perahu di dayung, dayung di perahu, perahu di dayung.
[9] The canoe is being rowed by Tayuruwiata, oar in canoe, the canoe is being rowed.

[10] *usiiayato namuji etemare bisini usiiayato*
[10] Daun pohon diatas pasir indah sekali.
[10] The tree-leaf on the sand is very beautiful,

[11] *namuji etemare tukuti i ayato pitinji*
[11] Senang sekali pohon kulit bagus.
[11] very pleasant is the good *kulit* tree (*kulit* = skin, bark).

[12] *itimare seepi tokote eayato pitiniji etemare*
[12] Ciptaan pinggir pohon bagus kulitnya.
[12] The image of the edge of the tree is its bark, very beautiful.

[13] *pitini ayato etemare ji ipi*
[13] itulah kulit bagus di atas kali Ji.
[13] It is the beautiful bark of the river Ji.

[14] *tokote iayato pitiniji etemare namini yoru*
[14] pohon bagus kulit bagus senang sekali.
[14] The good tree, the good bark is very enjoyed.

[15] *pari ja tamure yai pari je tamure nami yoru*
[15] Dayungnya perahu dayungnya anak perempuan.
[15] The oar of the boat is the one of a daughter.

[16] *pari ja tamunie yai pari ja tamuni tukuti iayoto*
[16] Tolong dayung perahu kayu bagus.
[16] Please row the good canoe.

[17] *pitini ji itimare se tokote yi ayato pitinji itimere.*
[17] Ciptaan dari kulit kayu bekas kulit.
[17] The image is of bark-wood, of used bark.

Stanza 24

[1] *Usiiayato saji nimi ite ainimare usiiayato sajiani*
[1] Daun kayu bagus seperti burung pombo putih. [Daun kayu bagus macam kampak
   bekas kampak. (M.)]
[1] The wood-leaf is beautiful, just like the white *pombo* bird. [The wood-leaf is as
   beautiful as an axe. (M.)]

[2] *mi jita jita ainimare bisini tuni usiiayato*
[2] Pohon di atas pasir indahnya seperti awan putih. [Kampak jalan-jalan di atas pasi.
   (M.)]
[2] The tree on the sand is beautiful, just like the white cloud, [The axe goes walking
   on the sand. (M.)]

[3] *sajianimi jita ainimare*
[3] seperti burung pombo putih. [Gayanya macam kampak. (M.)]
[3] like the white *pombo* bird. [The form the same as an axe. (M.)]

[4] *usiiayato saji nimi jita ainimare*
[4] Pohon-pohon itu pergi seperti awan. [Daun pohon macam kampak yang pergi.
   (M.)]
[4] Those trees move like clouds. [The tree-leaf is like a walking axe. (M.)]

[5] *bisini tuni usiwiayato sajia nimi jita jita*
[5] Pohon di atas pasir indah juga. [Pasir kayunya bagus macam kampak. (M.)]
[5] The tree on the sand is also beautiful. [The sawdust is as beautiful as an axe. (M.)]

[6] *ainimare usi iayato sajia ni mi jita jitaainimare*
[6] Daun pohon indah sekali di atas pasir. [Jalan sudah gaya kayu macam kampak. (M.)]
[6] The tree-leaf is very beautiful on the sand. [The walking is already the form like
   an axe. (M.)]

[7] *Tayuruwiata puja tama oranie*
[7] Tayuruwiata tolong dayung perahukah ?
[7] Tayuruwiata please help rowing the canoe.

[8] *Tayuruwiata puja tama oranie tipuje tama ora*
[8] Tayuruwiata tolong dayung saya punya perahu
[8] Tayuruwiata please help me rowing the canoe.

[9] *nie puja tama orania osei ayato namujie*
[9] saya senang sekali melihat indahnya pohon
[9] I enjoy very much seeing the beauty of the tree.

[10] *ainimare usiiayato sajianimi jita ainimare*

[10] begitu indahnya daun pohon di atas pasir

[10] So beautiful is the tree-leaf on the sand.

[11] *bisini tuni usiwi ayato sajiani mi jita ainimare*

[11] pohon di atas pasir bagaikan burung-burung

[11] The tree on the sand is like a bird.

[12] *usiwi ayato sajianimi jita ainimare*

[12] daun pohon seperti pombo putih

[12] The leaf of the tree is the same as the white *pombo* (bird).

[13] *bisini tuni usiwi ayato sajini juta ainimare*

[13] pohon di atas pasir bagaikan burung-burung

[13] The tree on the sand is like the bird.

[14] *Tayuruwiata puja tama orani tipuye tamaora*

[14] Tayuruwiata tolong dayung perahukah ?

[14] Tayuruwiata please help rowing the canoe.

[15] *nie pujetama oranie tukuti iayato bora nimi*

[15] karena daun pohon indah sekali

[15] As the leaf of the tree is very beautiful.

[16] *jita jita ainimare seipi tokote iayato boranimi*

[16] sambil jalan sambil pergi daun pohon itu

[16] While walking, while walking away is the leaf of the tree.

[17] *jita ainimare tukuti iayatu boranimi*

[17] sambil jalan sambil pergi daun pohon itu

[17] While walking, while walking away is the leaf of the tree.

[18] *juta juta ainimare seripi tukuti iayato*

[18] daun pohon seperti pombo putih

[18] The tree-leaf is the same as the white *pombo* (bird),

[19] *boranimi juta ainimare Naminiyoru pari*

[19] seperti Naminiyoru yang dayung di atas sana

[19] as Naminiyoru who rows up there.

60

[20] *jatama oranie yaipari ye tama orania.*

[20] gaya dayungnya juga seperti perempuan

[20] His way of rowing is the same as of a woman.

Stanza 25

[1] *Tayuruwiata mana waine Saunatu mana waine*

[1] Tayuruwiata mereka berkelahi Saunatu makan dia

[1] Tayuruwiata they fight themselves, Saunatu eats him.

[2] *Tayuruwiata mana waine bero mana*

[2] Tayuruwiata burung urip sedang makan buah-buah

[2] Tayuruwiata *urip* bird is just eating fruits.

[3] *waine bisini tuni bero mana waine*

[3] burung urip sedang menghadap sagu di pasir

[3] *Urip* bird is sago just standing on the sand opposite,

[4] *bero ayato isima dia enaomore bisini tuni*

[4] urip bagus ini warnanya merah-merahan

[4] this beautiful *urip* has a red colour.

[5] *bero ayato isima dia enaomare*

[5] urip burung indah sedang datang

[5] *Urip* is a beautiful bird, is just coming,

[6] *Berayaito isima dia enaomare bisini tuni.*

[6] urip yang di atas pasir indah sekali [Beraito dengan kulit merah-merah datang di atas pasir. (?)]

[6] *urip* which is on the sand is very beautiful. [Berayaito comes with reddened skin to the beach. (?)]

[7] *Beraitu isima die enaomare Beraito isima*

[7] merah-merahan yang datang urip itu [Beraito datang dengan kulit merah-merah, Beraito datang dengan kulit merah-merah (?)]

[7] The red one that comes is the *urip*, [Beraitu comes with reddened skin, Beraito comes with reddened skin. (?)]

[8] *dia enaumare bisini tuni Beraitu isima die*

[8] mari sedang datang sudah urip merah [Bapa datang di atas pasir. Beraito datang dengan kulit merah-merah (?)]

[8] Please that what is just coming up is the red *urip*. [Dad comes to the beach. Beraitu comes with reddened skin. (?)]

[9] *enaumare Tenaitu isima dia enaumare*

[9] sedang datang sudah pohon sagu di atas pasir [Tenaitu (=Beraito) datang dengan kulit merah-merah. (?)]

[9] He, the sago tree appears at the moment ready on the sand. [Tenaitu (=Beraito) comes with reddened skin. (?)]

[10] *bisini tuni Tenaitu isima dia enaumare*

[10] pohon sagu berbunga warna merah-merahan [Di atas pasir Tenaitu datang dengan kulit merah. (?)]

[10] The sago tree blossoms in red colour. [To the beach comes Tenaitu with reddened skin. (?)]

[11] *Tayuruwiata mana waina bero mana waine*

[11] Tayuruwiata sedang menarik perhatian orang [Tayuruwiata main mata dengan Bero, main mata. (?)]

[11] Tayuruwiata is just drawing the attention of the people to her. [Tayuruwiata twinkles with Bero, twinkles. (?)]

[12] *Tayuruwiata mana waina bisini mana waine*

[12] Tayuruwiata yang di atas pasir itu suka perhatikan orang [Tayuruwiata main mata dengan pasir, main mata. (?)]

[12] Tayuruwiata who is on the sand enjoys the attention of the other one. [Tayuruwiata twinkles with the beach, twinkles. (?)]

[13] *bisini tuni mana waina Beroayato isima dia enaomare*

[13] di atas pasir urip itu merah-merahan [Di atas pasir ia main mata, Beraito datang dengan kulit merah-merah (?)]

[13] On the sand is the red *urip*. [On the beach Beroayato twinkles, comes with reddened skin. (?)]

[14] *Tenawaitu isima dia enaumare bisini*

[14] di atas pasir pohon sagu merah-merahan [Teniitu dengan kulit merah-merah datang di atas pasir (?)]

[14] On the sand is the red sago tree. [Tenawaitu with reddened skin comes to the beach. (?)]

62

[15] *tuni Tenaitu isima die enaomare Yunut aya*
[15] merah-merahan pohon di atas pasir [Teniitu datang dengan kulit merah-merah. (?)]
[15] Red is the tree on the sand. [Tenaitu comes with reddened skin. (?)]

[16] *tu kamu ma dia enaomare Yunut ayatu kamuma*
[16] sagu juga di atas pasir merah [Yunut datang dengan kulit merah-merah. (?)]
[16] Sago is also red on the sand. [Yunut comes with reddened skin. (?)]

[17] *die enaomare kamuma dia enaomare sene*
[17] merah-merahan pohon di atas pasir [Datang dengan kulit merah-merah, datang. (?)]
[17] Red is the tree on the sand. [Comes with reddened skin, comes. (?)]

[18] *sene tuni ka mu ma dia enaomare Naminiyoru*
[18] air di kali juga ikut berwarna merah [Di atas pasir datang dengan kulit merah-merah. (?)]
[18] The water of the river also comes with the red, [To the beach comes with the reddened skin. (?)]

[19] *amai waine amai waine Naminiyorra*
[19] di malam hari Naminiyoru air di kali berwarna merah [Naminiyoru main mata, main mata (?)]
[19] at night Naminiyoru the water in the river is red. [Naminiyoru twinkles, twinkles. (?)]

[20] *amai waine amai waine seni tuni amai*
[20] perahu itu juga langsung dayung terus [Naminiyoru main mata, main mata di atas pasir. (?)]
[20] The canoe is also directly rowed on [Naminiyorra twinkles, twinkles on the beach. (?)]

[21] *waina Yunutaitu kamuma dia enaumare*
[21] menuju ke tempat pasir merah-merahan [Yunutaitu datang kulit merah-merah. (?)]
[21] to the place of the red sand. [Yunutaitu comes with reddened skin. (?)]

[22] *Yunutayatu kamuma dia enaomare sene*
[22] [Yunutaitu datang dengan kulit merah-merah di atas pasir. (?)]
[22] [Yunutayatu comes with reddened skin to the beach. (?)]

[23] *tuni Yunutayatu kamuma die enaomare*
[23] [Yunutaitu datang dengan kulit merah-merah. (?)]
[23] [Yunutayatu comes with reddened skin. (?)]

Stanza 26

[1] *Wanawata biva uma pua umisimare tibiva*
[1] [Wanawata ambil air isi di perahu. (?)]
[1] [Wanawata draws water and fills the canoe. (?)]

[2] *uma po umisimare Wanawata biva uma pua umisimare*
[2] [Ki air di perahu. Wanawata ambil air isi di perahu. (?)]
[2] [Fills water into the canoe. Wanawata draws and fills water into the canoe. (?)]

[3] *tibiva uma pua umisimare uma pua*
[3] [Ambil air isi di perahu, ambil air isi di perahu. (?)]
[3] [Draws the water and fills into the canoe, draws the water and fills into the canoe. (?)]

[4] *umisimare tibi uma pua umisimare tibiva*
[4] [Ambil air isi di perahu, ambil isi di perahu. (?)]
[4] [Draws the water and fills into the canoe, draws the water and fills into the canoe. (?)]

[5] *uma pua umisimare dati putaka siri yapua umisimare*
[5] [Isi air di perahu, perahu kami tidak baik. Karena siri=iri hati (?)]
[5] [Fills the water into the canoe, canoe is not good because of the jealousy. (?)]

[6] *yapu putaka siri yapua umisimare dati*
[6] [Dayung kamu tidak baik. Iri hati (tidak senang). (?)]
[6] [Your oar is not good, jealousy (unhappy). (?)]

[7] *putaka siri yapua umisimare yapu putakava*
[7] [Perahu kamu tidak baik. Tidak senang. Dayung kamu tidak baik (?)]
[7] [Your oar is not good, unhappy. Your oar is not good. (?)]

[8] *ompe simi yapua umisimare Wanauta*
[8] [Dayung kamu tidak baik, kata mereka. (?)]
[8] [Your oar is not good, they say. (?)]

[9] *biva uma pua wimisimare. Ti bi uma puaumisimare*
[9] [Wanauta ambil air isi di perahu. (?)]
[9] [Wanauta draws the water and fills it into the canoe.]

¹⁰ *Wanauta biva uma puaumisimare*
¹⁰ [Ambil air isi di perahu. Wanauta ambil air isi di perahu. (?)]
¹⁰ [Draws the water fills into the canoe. Wanauta draws the water fills into the canoe. (?)]

¹¹ *ti biva uma puaumisimare ti putakafa umi*
¹¹ [Ambil air isi di perahu. Perahu tidak baik, kata mereka (?)]
¹¹ [Draws the water fills into the canoe. The canoe is not good, they say. (?)]

¹² *pesimia ya pua umisimare pu putakafa*
¹² [Kata orang, dayung kamu tidak baik. (?)]
¹² [They say, your oar is not good. (?)]

¹³ *umipesimi ya pua umisimare du pari putakafa*
¹³ [Dayung kamu tidak baik. Dayung kamu tidak baik. (?)]
¹³ [Your oar is not good. Your oar is not good. (?)]

¹⁴ *umipesimia dayai putakafa umi pesi mia yapua*
¹⁴ [Dayung kamu tidak baik. Perahu kamu tidak baik (?)]
¹⁴ [Your oar is not good. Your canoe is not good. (?)]

¹⁵ *isimi Saunatu vaka yai tisima pua isimia*
¹⁵ [Dengan bambu Saunatu bongkar Yai yang tidak baik. (?)]
¹⁵ [With bamboo Saunatu pulls down the bad ritual house. (?)]

¹⁶ *yai okamifa uma pua umisimare*
¹⁶ [Ambil air isi di perahu (?)]
¹⁶ [draws the water, fills the canoe. (?)]

¹⁷ *Naminiyoru okami yai umapua umisimare*
¹⁷ [Naminiyoru ambil air isi di perahu. (?)]
¹⁷ [Naminiyoru draws the water, fills the canoe. (?)]

¹⁸ *puaumisimare yai ukamima umapua umisimare*
¹⁸ [Mereka jalan sambil isi air di perahu, ambil air isi di perahu. (?)]
¹⁸ [They ride and during that fills the water into the canoe, draws the water, fills into the canoe. (?)]

¹⁹ *yai okamifa umapua umisimare*
¹⁹ [air di perahu karena banyak orang. (?)]
¹⁹ [Water in the canoe because there are many people. (?)]

[20] yaka yai putakafa pesimia yapua umisimare

[20] [Perahu kamu tidak baik, kata orang perahu kamu tidak baik. (?)]

[20] [Your canoe is not good. They say your canoe is not good. (?)]

[21] yaka pari putakafa pesimia yapua umisimare

[21] [Dayung kamu tidak baik, kata orang dayung kamu tidak baik. (?)]

[21] [Your oar is not good. They say your oar is not good. (?)]

Stanza 27

[1] Dia sarama utinimare beta sarama utinimare

[1] Bapa ikut dari belakang – ikut dari belakang [Bapa ikut dari belakang, ikut dari belakang. (?)]

[1] Father comes from behind, comes from behind, [Dad follows from behind, follows from behind, (?)]

[2] asapifa sarama utinimare asapifa sarama

[2] ikut dari belakang jalan dari belakang [Ikut dari belakang ikut dari belakang (?)]

[2] comes from behind, goes from behind. [follows from behind, follows from behind. (?)]

[3] utinimare Bintua sarama utinimare asapifa

[3] ikut di belakang sarang ular Bintutua [Bintu ikut dari belakang (?)]

[3] Afterwards comes the nest of the snake Bintutua, [Bintu comes behind, (?)]

[4] sarama witinimare asapifa sarama utinimare.

[4] dari belakang ikut dia dari belakang [ikut dari belakang - ikut dari belakang (?)]

[4] comes after him from behind. [comes afterwards, comes afterwards. (?)]

[5] Yuri tia bapai mete bapai meteesori

[5] muka dari perahu harus dibalik [Yuri perut kembali – perut kembali sori(?)]

[5] The front part of the canoe has to be turned around, [Yuri belly comes back, does Sori come back? (?)]

[6] tia bapai mitia bapaya mitie

[6] balik muka dan balik perut [perut cembali - perut kembali (?)]

[6] Front part turn around and the stomach. [Belly comes back, belly comes back. (?)]

[7] *Yuri bapai mitia bapai mitie Soiri tia bapai*
[7] balik muka di sini Souri punya perut [Yuri kembali, kembali. Soiri kembali. (?)]
[7] The front part turns around here, Souri has belly, [Yuri come back, come back. Soiri comes back. (?)]

[8] *metie. Yuri au sarama utinimare asapifa*
[8] dari belakang ia jalan terus [Yuri ikut dari belakang (?)]
[8] from behind he goes on. [Yuri come from behind. (?)]

[9] *sarama witinimare Sori au sarama utinimare*
[9] dari belakang Souri berjalan kaki terus [Dia ikut dari belakang. Soiri ikut dari belakang (?)]
[9] From behind Souri walks on. [He follows from behind. Soiri comes, follows from behind. (?)]

[10] *asapifa sarama utinimare tia bapaya*
[10] di belakang pergi tapi balik muka [Ikut dari belakang. Kembali (?)]
[10] But the backside goes, turns the front-side around. [Follows from behind, comes back. (?)]

[11] *mitia bafira mitie Pasutu bafirami tia bafira*
[11] muka juga harus dibalik perut juga [Kembali Pasutu (=Yuri) kembali. (?)]
[11] The front-side also has to be turned around also the belly, [Pasutu (=Yuri) come back, come. (?)]

[12] *mitie Pasutu bafira emete bapaya emete*
[12] anjing juga harus dibalik pulang [Kembali Pasutu kembali. Kembali. (?)]
[12] the dog has to be given back. [Pasutu come back, come back, come back. (?)]

[13] *ani asarama utinimare Sori ausarama*
[13] kabar tentang Souri tersebat ke mana-mana [Ani (?) ikut dari belakang, Sori ikut dari belakang. (?)]
[13] The welfare over Souri is spread everywhere. [Ani (?) follows from behind. Sori follows from behind. (?)]

[14] *utinimare Pasutu ausarama utinimare*
[14] anjing dari belakang juga pergi [Pasutu ikut dari belakang. (?)]
[14] The dog from behind also accompanies. [Pasutu follows from behind. (?)]

[15] *Sori asapiva sarama witinimare Pasutu*
[15] Souri ikut anjing dari belakang [Soiri ikut dari belakang. Pasutu kembali. (?)]
[15] Souri follows the dog from behind, [Soiri follows from behind. Pasutu comes
    back. (?)]

[16] *bavira imi te bavira emete Sori bavira emete*
[16] betul perempuan ini bagus Souri [Kembali. Sori cembali (?)]
[16] really this woman is beautiful, Souri. [Come back, Sori come back (?)]

[17] *Pasutu bavira emet tameni. Asarama utinimare*
[17] anjing ramai sekali di depan [Pasutu, engkau kembali. Ikut dari belakang (?)]
[17] The dog in front is very loud, [Pasutu you come back, follow from behind. (?)]

[18] *Sori asapiva sarama utinimare*
[18] dari belakang Souri ikut [Soiri ikut dari belakang (?)]
[18] behind Souri accompanies. [Soiri follows from behind (?)]

[19] *Pasutu ausarama utinimare Pasutu*
[19] anjing juga harus dibalik pulang [Pasutu ikut. Pasutu ikut (?)]
[19] The dog has to be sent home, [Pasutu follows from behind. Pasutu follows (?)]

[20] *asapifa sarama utinimare.*
[20] dari belakang (Souri) berjalan kaki terus. [dari belakang. (?)]
[20] from behind (Souri) walks on. [from behind. (?)]

Stanza 28

[1] *Tayuruwiata duru utanimi jima usarami*
[1] Tayuruwiata engkau pergi ke mana [Tayuruwiata engkau mau bikin apa untuk
    saya. (?)]
[1] Tayuruwiata, where are you going to, [Tayuruwiata, what do you want to do for
    me? (?)]

[2] *jima usarame Naminiyoru duru utanimi*
[2] mau bagaimana Naminiyoru ini [Mau bikin apa. Naminiyoru engkau mau bikin
    apa. (?)]
[2] what did this Naminiyoru want? [What do you want to do Naminiyoru, what do
    you want to do? (?)]

[3] *yursausanimi yursausanimi*

[3] lompat pergi ke sebelah kali sana [Bikin apa untuk saya, bikin apa untuk saya. (?)]

[3] Go to the other side of the river to jump. [What do you want to do for me, what do you want to do for me? (?)]

[4] *Tayuruwiata duru utanimi ima usanimi*

[4] Tayuruwiata dari sebab apa engkau datang [Tayuruwiata engkau mau bikin apa untuk saya. (?)]

[4] Tayuruwiata, for what reason are you coming? Tayuruwiata, where are you going to? [Tayuruwiata, what do you want to do for me? (?)]

[5] *jima usa nimie Saunatu duru amta umi*

[5] Saunatu datang ambil saya juga [Engkau mau bikin apa saya Saunatu. Saya mau bawa (?)]

[5] Saunatu comes also to fetch me. [What do you want to do for me Saunatu. I (Tayuruwiata) want to take with me. (?)]

[6] *ira bainia Tamatapis tami ama ni fa amta*

[6] bawa saya juga ke rumah Tamutapis [Engkau ke dalam rumah Tamutapis (?)]

[6] Bring me also to the house Tamutapis, [You go into the house Tamutapis. (?)]

[7] *umi ira bainie amra umiira baindie*

[7] datang ambil saya juga [Saya bawa engkau, saya bawa engkau (?)]

[7] come also to fetch me. [I take you with me, I take you. (?)]

[8] *Saunatu duru amra umi ira baindie*

[8] Saunatu ikut dari belakang saja [Saunatu nanti saya akan bawa engkau. (?)]

[8] Saunatu just comes from behind. [Saunatu, I shall take you with me. (?)]

[9] *amta umi ira baindie Tamatapisi yai amanifa*

[9] saya akan membawa engkau ke kampung Tamutapis [Saya akan bawa engkau ke dalam Yai Tamutapis (?)]

[9] I shall take you to the village Tamutapis, [I shall take you into the *yai* Tamutapis with me. (?)]

[10] *amta umi ira baindie. Sawini duru uta*

[10] bawa saya tetapi jangan Sawini sendiri [Saya akan bawa engkau. Sawini saya (?)]

[10] bring me there, but not only Sawini, [I shall take you with me, my Sawini (?)]

[11] *nimi yursa seri yursa serie*

[11] harus anjing dibawa semua [Kenapa begitu kenapa begitu Naminiyoru (?)]

[11] all dogs have to be taken along. [Why is this that way, why is it so, Naminiyoru? (?)]

[12] *Namiminiyoru duutamimi yursausanimi yursausanimi*

[12] Naminiyoru engkau buat saya bagaimana [Saya kenapa begitu begitu. (?)]

[12] Naminiyoru, how have you made me? [Why am I once that way then the other way? (?)]

[13] *Sawini duru ataberaumiira baindie*

[13] Sawini biar bawa saya juga pergi ke sana [Sawini nanti saya bawa engkau (?)]

[13] Sawini, take me also to go with you to there. [Sawini, I shall take you with me. (?)]

[14] *Sawini duru utanimi yursa senimia*

[14] Sawini engkau mau tinggalkan saya [Sawini saya kenapa begitu (?)]

[14] Sawini, you wanted to leave me. [Why is my Sawini once that way then the other way? (?)]

[15] *akutamanifa amta umiira baindie Yiapisi*

[15] Jiapisi (=perempuau-perempuan roh) ikut dengan engkau [Dalam Yai bawa engkau Yiapisi. (?)]

[15] Jiapisi (spirits of women) come with you. [In the *yai* takes you Yiapisi with him. (?)]

[16] *akut amanifa amta umiira baindie*

[16] biar bawa saya ikut pergi ke sana [Dalam Yai bawa engkau. (?)]

[16] Take me with you to go there, [Into the *yai* you with him. (?)]

[17] *amra wimi ira baindia yiapisi akut amanifa*

[17] bawa Jiapisi ke atas kali potong untuk bawa [Bawa masuk engkau Yiapisi dalam Yai (?)]

[17] bring Jiapisi to the connecting river to take her with you. [Takes you, Yiapisi, into the *yai*. (?)]

[18] *amta umiira baindie Naminiyoru duru*

[18] bawa saya pergi juga bersama Naminiyoru [Bawa masuk engkau Naminiyoru saya. (?)]

[18] Take me also with you, together with Naminiyoru go to there, [bring you in, my Naminiyoru. (?)]

[19] *utanimi yursaserie isausa nimi isausa*

[19] bagaimana bawa saya atau tidak [Kenapa begitu - begitu - begitu (?)]

[19] who is it, take me with you or not. [Why once that way, then the other way? (?)]

[20] *nimie Naminyoru duru utani mi yursa*

[20] Naminiyoru mau buat saya bagaimana [Naminiyoru saya kenapa begitu (?)]

[20] What did Naminiyoru want to do with me? [Why is my Naminiyoru once that
way then the other way? (?)]

[21] *usa nimia isra usa nimie Sawini amta*

[21] saya akan bawa engkau ke dunia sana Sawini [Kenapa begitu Sawini bawa (?)]

[21] I want to bring you Sawini to the other world, [Why take Sawini that way? (?)]

[22] *utinira baindie Yiapisi akut amanifa amta*

[22] saya akan bawa engkau ke Jiapisi [nanti bawa engkau Yiapisi dalam Yai (=Akut). (?)]

[22] I want to take you to Jiapisi, [will take you into the *yai* Yiapisi? (?)]

[23] *witinira baindie Yiwi amta witinira baindie*

[23] mau ikut bersama ke sana bersamamu dia juga [bawa engkau Yiwi bawa engkau. (?)]

[23] want to come there together also with him. [take you Yiwi with me, take you with
me. (?)]

Stanza 29

[1] *Ayeesemere Tamatapisi imi yani yawimi*

[1] Sepanjang hari Tamutapis teriak terus [Gembira malam hari Tamutapis tifa bunyi
(?)]

[1] Every day Tamutapis continues screaming. [Cheerful in the evening, Tamutapis,
the sound of drums. (?)]

[2] *simare aye wimi simare Tamatapisi imi yani*

[2] Tamutapis ikut di dalam pesta di sana [Goyang gembira malam hari, Tamutapis
tifa bunyi. (?)]

[2] Tamutapis comes to the feast there. [Dance cheerful in the evening, Tamutapis, the
sound of drums. (?)]

³ Wa yani nimi iaumisimare jaumisimare

³ ada bunyi terus ada bunyi ribut [macam bunyi ombak gembira malam hari
  (yaumisimare), gembira malam hari (yaumisimare) (?)]

³ There is always sound, there is noise. [Just like the rustle of a wave, cheerful in
  the evening, cheerful in the evening. (?)]

⁴ Saunatu yani yukue Saunatu yani yuku

⁴ Saunatu dengar bunyi Saunatu dengar bunyi [Saunatu pasang telinga. Saunatu
  pasang telinga. (?)]

⁴ Saunatu hears the sound, Saunatu hears the sound, [Saunatu fixes his ear on, fixes
  his ear on. (?)]

⁵ jare Saunatu yani juku ja warae

⁵ cepat Saunatu diam ya di mana-mana [Saunatu pasang telinga engkau (?)]

⁵ be quiet, quickly Saunatu, yes everywhere. [Saunatu fix your ear on. (?)]

⁶ yani yuku jaoraa

⁶ coba dengar [pasang telinga. (?)]

⁶ Listen please. [Fix your ear on (?)]

⁷ auja umisimare Tamatapisi imi yani wa

⁷ Tamutapis sedang asyik menjaring [Gembira malam hari Tamutapisi tifa bunyi. (?)]

⁷ Tamutapis is just fishing enthusiastically. [Cheerful in the evening Tamutapisi, the
  sound of drums. (?)]

⁸ yanimi jaumisimare auja esemare Tamatapisi

⁸ bunyi sekarang datang karena Tamutapis [Seperti bunyi ombak gembira malam
  hari Tamatapisi (?)]

⁸ The sound now comes because of Tamutapis. [Just like the rustle of the wave,
  cheerful in the evening, Tamatapisi. (?)]

⁹ imi jani wa yania nimi jaumisimare

⁹ mereka pukul tifa macam bunyi ombak [tapis tifa bunyi seperti ombak gembira
  malam hari (?)]

⁹ They beat the drum like the sound of the wave. [The sound of the drum like a
  wave, cheerful in the evening. (?)]

^{10} *Saunatu yani yuku jara Saunatu yani juku*
^{10} Saunatu senang dengar Saunatu sedang dengar [Saunatu pasang telinga engkau
    pasang telinga. (?)]
^{10} Saunatu likes to hear it, Saunatu hears it at the moment. [Saunatu fix your ear on,
    fix your ear, (?)]

^{11} *jarai Sawini kinifi yuku jarai sauna*
^{11} bunyi tifa didengar Sawini seperti bunyi ombak [engkau Sawini pasang telinga. (?)]
^{11} The voice of the drum was heard by Sawini, just like the sound of the wave. [you
    Sawini fix your ear on, (?)]

^{12} *kinifi yuku jara Sauna kinifi yuku jarai*
^{12} Saunat pasang telinga baik-baik bunyi apa [Engkau Saunat pasang telinga engkau
    Saunat pasang telinga (?)]
^{12} Saunat fixes his ears attentively on which voice? [you Saunat fix your ear, you
    Saunat fix your ear. (?)]

^{13} *auja esemara Jiapisi bataru yana jaumisimare*
^{13} perempuan hamil juga ikut hadir [gembira malam hari Jiapisi tifa bunyi (?)]
^{13} The pregnant woman is also present. [Cheerful in the evening, Jiapisi, the sound
    of drums. (?)]

^{14} *auja esemara Jiapisi bataruyana*
^{14} coba ambil saya karena di sini ada saya [gembira malam hari Jiapisi tifa bunyi. (?)]
^{14} Try once to fetch me, as I am here. [Cheerful in the evening, Jiapisi, the sound of
    drums. (?)]

^{15} *basu yanie nimi yaumisimare auja esemare*
^{15} ambil saya sambil sepanjang malam hari [Seperti bunyi ombak di malam hari (?)]
^{15} Fetch me the whole night through. [Just like the rustle of the wave in the evening. (?)]

^{16} *Jiapisi bataru yana basuyani nimi*
^{16} Jiapisi harus kita ambil [Gembira malam hari Jiapisi bunyi tifa (?)]
^{16} We have to fetch Jiapisi [Cheerful in the evening, Jiapisi, the sound of drums. (?)]

^{17} *jaesemare.*
^{17} malam ini juga. [Seperti bunyi ombak di malam hari. (?)]
^{17} tonight. [Just like the rustle of the wave in the evening. (?)]

3

Index